TAX-FREE

2000

The Rebirth of American Liberty

Dr. Murray Sabrin

Prescott Press
Lafayette, LA

Prescott Press
P.O. Box 53777
Lafayette, LA 70505

Library of Congress Card Catalog Number:
94-065023
ISBN: 0-933451-25-3

Dedication

To Flor,

who made it all possible.

Contents

Contents

Preface

Tax -Free 2000: The Rebirth of American Liberty was written during the fall of 1992 at the height of the presidential campaign. While I was writing the initial draft of the manuscript, virtually all the economic fallacies I was criticizing were being presented to the American people by George Bush, Bill Clinton, and Ross Perot on their campaign trails. The three candidates, instead of addressing the most fundamental issue of our time—what are the responsibilities of government?— asserted that in general government can solve the nation's problems by being more efficient, or more "compassionate." None of the major candidates, however, blamed the mess in Washington and the pain on Main Street on the institutions and programs that have become the country's sacred cows—the Federal Reserve, paper money, Social Security, the income tax, and public education—that is, government intervention.

Although it was tempting to write opinion-editorial pieces or a letter to the editor to point out that the economic IQ of the major presidential candidates left much to be desired, the completion of the manuscript was my priority then, just as the distribution of *Tax-Free 2000* is now.

The election of Bill Clinton—and the implementation of his economic program—has markedly accelerated government intervention in the American people's lives. We, the American people, therefore have to decide if we want to travel on the road to bigger and bigger government, or if we want to establish a free economy. This is the challenge we face as we are about to enter the twenty-first century.

As the twentieth century draws to a close, several observations about the past one hundred years are in order. Socialism/communism was a great failure—it could not deliver goods to the people—and was an incredibly brutal system. The welfare state failed in England and Sweden, the two Western nations that embraced welfarism with a passion. Finally, the mixed economies (United States, Western Europe, and Japan) are on the brink of a major crisis. Only time will tell whether the market-oriented democracies can avoid an economic upheaval or a financial meltdown. Before we can correct the ills that face our country, the American people need to understand why the mixed economy is unworkable.

Tax-Free 2000 was written to explain, inform, and educate the American people about the dangers of governmental power and the consequences of economic intervention. Once we realize that government power is the enemy of both sustainable prosperity and personal freedom, we can then swiftly dismantle America's welfare state.

The American dream, the great achievements of individual Americans, is not now in jeopardy. Hundreds of thousands of Americans are becoming successful entrepreneurs, entertainers, athletes, writers, etc. The American dream that is in jeopardy is the country's economic and social stability. We cannot afford, as a nation, to succumb to an economic upheaval. An America in turmoil would have dire consequences for the future prosperity of the nation and the people's personal freedom.

Tax-Free 2000 constitutes a banquet for the American people to feast upon. The first two chapters are the appetizers. Munching on them should get you so angry about how our ancestors were treated by kings, caesars, lords, presidents, and other scoundrels throughout history, that any faith you may still have in smiling governmental officials who promise us security should be dispelled quickly.

That we Americans from different parts of the globe are alive today, given all that our ancestors went through for the past five thousand years, is a miracle. It makes you wonder what the world would be like today if freedom and liberty had reigned throughout history instead of coercion and tyranny.

Since we cannot turn back the hands of time, we must, however, understand the nature of the *beast*—big government. Chapters 3 through 6 explain how government is undermining sustainable prosperity and in the process eroding our basic freedoms. In chapters 7 and 8, the last dish of the banquet, a roadmap to a free economy is drawn. If we take this road, our descendants will thank us for establishing the kind of society the founding fathers envisioned more than 200 years ago.

For dessert, the epilogue tops off the meal. If you want to know why a tax-free America is achievable, don't forget this dessert!

Tax-Free 2000 was a joy to write after twenty years of studying economics, finance, history, and philosophy. If the American people concur with my understanding of what makes a good society, then I am wildly optimistic about the country's future. If a majority of the American people continue to believe in "free lunches," "Santa Claus," and the "tooth fairy," then they will deserve the consequences of their fantasies. For those of us, however, who believe that free enterprise is better than a mixed economy, we will continue to fight for the principles of extremely limited government and *laissez-faire*.

I've gathered the ingredients and "prepared the banquet." So enjoy the meal . . . it may be the most important one of your life.

--Murray Sabrin

Acknowledgments

This book is a synthesis of hundreds of books, monographs, and articles I have read during the past twenty-five years. I thus owe a debt of gratitude to several individuals—deceased and living—who paved the way for both the foundation and framework of *Tax-Free 2000* to be constructed. These include Frederic Bastiat, Frank Chodorov, Ludwig von Mises, Henry Hazlitt, Robert Higgs, Ron Paul, Lewis Lehrman, James Payne, and Charles Adams. I owe a special debt of gratitude to Professor Murray N. Rothbard, S. J. Hall Distinguished Professor of Economics at the University of Nevada, Las Vegas, who was a member of my dissertation committee when I attended Rutgers University. His extraordinary output of books, monographs and articles has had an enormous influence on my understanding of economics, history, and political philosophy.

I would like to thank several individuals who read all or parts of the manuscript and made cogent comments and suggestions: Teresa Hutchins, Sheldon Richman, and Joseph Salerno. Leonard Liggio's many insightful comments and his suggestions for additional material about the history of taxation were especially helpful. Robert McGee not only offered many worthwhile suggestions, he also demonstrated his keen editing skills. Gratitude also goes to Aggie Kolek, an extraordinary student, who assisted me by gathering material for several chapters.

I am grateful to the Vice President for Academic Affairs office at Ramapo College for granting me a sabbatical to pursue this project. The manuscript was typed by an incredibly able and efficient trio of secretaries in the School of Administration and Business, Kathy Zdrodowski, Joan McCaffrey, and Marie Vojitovitz, who also coordinated the project. Kathy deserves special mention for typing the original draft and virtually all the subsequent changes, which must have seemed endless to her. For her dedication above and beyond the call of duty, she deserves more thanks than I can ever repay. I also would like to thank Sebastian Raciti and Richard Bond, Director and Acting Director, respectively, of the School of Administration and Business, for their encouragement and support while I was on sabbatical.

I would like to thank my parents, who know firsthand the impact of tyranny as Holocaust survivors, for instilling in me a love of learning at a very early age. This project bears the fruit of their efforts.

Also, I would like to thank Michael Harrison of TALKERS magazine and host of the syndicated radio show, "The Top Ten Radio Countdown," for inviting me on his show several times to discuss the country's economic conditions. A special thanks goes to Ray Masters of the Poconos libertarian discussion group for inviting me to present the outline of *Tax-Free 2000* to his members in 1991.

David H. England, editor-in-chief at Prescott Press, Inc. deserves special thanks for considering and accepting my manuscript for publication. Deserved recognition goes to Kay Walters, managing editor, and her staff of Dana Girod, Dean Shapiro, and Stephanie Morgan for their competent editing of the manuscript.

I could not have written *Tax-Free 2000* without the support of my wife, Florence, whom I've been with for twenty seven years (it doesn't seem that long). She made it possible for me to study for a doctorate full-time in the 1970s. My graduate studies allowed me to pursue my interest in economics, history, and finance, which eventually led to my college teaching career. In addition, for the past two years, Florence indulged my pursuit of this project by foregoing substantial leisure time while I worked on *Tax-Free 2000*. Florence also read and corrected several drafts of the manuscript. As a layman when it comes to economics, she offered many insightful comments that improved the final draft.

Needless to say, despite all the talented individuals who read the manuscript, any errors remain my responsibility.

Introduction

Self-preservation and self-development are common aspirations among all people. And if everyone enjoyed the unrestricted use of his faculties and the free disposition of the fruits of his labor, social progress would be ceaseless, uninterrupted, and unfailing.

--Frederic Bastiat

The current debate over the federal government's economic policies revolves around one primary issue. How much should spending increase in the next fiscal year? The squabble between the Democrats and Republicans is whether the federal government's expenditures should increase substantially (the Democrats' goal) or "only" 5 percent or less (the Republicans' response). No one in Congress is calling for the federal budget to be *reduced*, that is, for the federal government to spend *less* money in the next fiscal year than in previous years. In short, both major political parties assume that the federal government should spend, tax, and borrow in order to redistribute income and deliver various services to the American people. In essence, the Democrats want a comprehensive welfare state come hell or high water while the Republicans want an "efficient" welfare state. After all, the Republicans are pro-business.

The contemporary theory of government is that we, the people, need a multitude of services that only government can provide and that transferring income to tens of millions of Americans is a legitimate function of government. Both propositions are untenable. Virtually every service the government—federal, state, or local—provides the American people has been—or could be—provided by the private sector. Transferring income is a euphemism for massive legal plunder and should end immediately.

The goal of *Tax-Free 2000* is to refocus the public discussion about taxation and the role of government in society. *Tax-Free 2000* presents a vision of government for the American people to consider. Instead of tax and spend, tax and borrow, *Tax-Free 2000* proposes that the United States embrace Bastiat's insight, namely that the people should have total control over the fruits of their labor so they can create a sustainable prosperity. A sustainable prosperity is not possible as long as government spends and taxes. Make no mistake about it, if taxes and government spending were the key to sustainable prosperity, we would be witnessing a global boom. Government spending is at or approaching unprecedented levels throughout the industrialized world, and not surprisingly, stagnation, high unemployment, and massive budget deficits have been the inevitable results. The key to economic growth, however, is for government to confine itself to an important role in society, protecting people and their property from aggression and theft. The unleashing of the private sector therefore will create greater wealth and more jobs—guaranteed.

Government has usurped the private sector's provision of numerous activities claiming the market, free enterprise, could not, should not, or would not, meet the people's needs. But, there is only one objective method to determine if a product or service should be produced or offered in the marketplace: can it be made available without subsidies, i.e., monies coerced from both employees and employers? The free market—the voluntary transactions between people—determines which goods and services should be produced while government purchases of goods and services reflect the demands of special interests for social programs. (Military expenditures are also inflated to support a military-industrial complex that is larger than necessary to protect the American people from foreign aggressors.) Producing goods and delivering services without a free market guarantees that the output of goods and services will not represent what the people want.

On the free market, *voluntary* exchanges reflect how resources should be allocated to produce the goods consumers desire most. In contemporary America, the free market provides for a wide variety of goods and services from discount retailers like K Mart to upscale chains like Nordstrom's. But, the current philosophical fad is *egalitarianism*, the belief that every American is entitled to an array of services regardless of income. This idea is an example of "soft" socialism, as opposed to the "hard" Socialist ideology which was responsible for the collapse of the former Soviet Union and its satellites. Although the United States and our trading partners are light years from the former Communist nations' economic policies, there are, however, too many similarities.

As shocking as it may sound, "socialism" was established in the United States in 1913, four years before the Bolshevik revolution in Russia, transforming America from a relatively *laissez-faire* (a hands-off approach of business by government) economy into the United Socialist States of America, USSA. Clearly, America did not embrace the tyrannical, totalitarian variety of socialism that engulfed Russia and her adjoining republics, which eventually became the Soviet Union, the U.S.S.R. The "revolution" of 1913 established a "mild" socialism in the United States, and a "mixed" economy, which gave the federal government substantial control over the economy. Instead of owning the means of production as in a fully socialized economy, the federal government, since 1913, has greatly influenced how the economy's output has been allocated. In short, the United States undertook a comprehensive social experiment, the welfare state. After eighty years, the results were in, the redistributive state (socialism with a smile) has been a colossal failure.

The adoption of the Sixteenth Amendment to the U.S. Constitution in February 1913 allowed the federal government to levy a direct tax on personal income and opened the way for the people's earnings to be plundered by Washington. The amendment in effect permitted the federal government to have an unlimited claim on the people's incomes. That the Congress has not authorized the IRS to take 100 percent of an individual's income is small comfort to the American people!

The possibility that the federal government could confiscate all the American people's earnings should be of concern to all lovers of liberty and economic freedom. The income tax puts too much power in the hands of the state and violates a fundamental principle of the revolution of 1776—that government is to protect the people from aggression and should not plunder the citizenry. In early 1913, therefore, one phase of America's counterrevolution was complete. The initial federal income tax exempted 98 percent of all Americans and was levied on only the very wealthy, who were supposed to pay *all* income taxes in the future. Currently, virtually every working American pays the income tax, and tens of millions of Americans are subject to marginal tax rates that even the most gung-ho proponents of the income tax in 1913 would probably find reprehensible. Not surprisingly, the income tax has become the most hated "institution" in the country, while the 15th of April is by far the most detested date of the year. Even politicians have been quoted as saying "no one likes the income tax." If no one likes the income tax (a greater understatement has never been made), then why are the American people subject to this coerced levy?

The second phase of America's plunge into "mild" socialism came in December 1913 when President Wilson signed the Federal Reserve Act, creating the Federal Reserve

System. The purpose of the Federal Reserve was ostensibly to stabilize the nation's banking system in order to prevent financial panics and deep depressions. In reality, the Fed was created so the nation's large commercial banks could inflate together so there would be a steady stream of newly created money and credit flowing from the central bank to the nation's banking system and then to the business community. In its role as the government's bank and "lender of last resort," banks would have "protection" of the mighty government in Washington, D.C., and therefore the banking system would be immunized from the panics that gripped the nation in the past. In short, the banks' risks would be "socialized," with the Federal Reserve ready to print money to bail out banks that engaged in imprudent lending practices.

The federal government's establishment of "monetary socialism" in the United States cannot be denied. Sound money means using a valuable commodity to facilitate exchanges. Historically, many commodities have been used as a general medium of exchange (money)—salt, copper, bronze, gold, silver, and tobacco. The marketplace, that is people engaging in voluntary exchanges, has determined which good(s) would best facilitate exchanges for other goods and services. From gold and silver coins, bank notes and bank drafts (checks) redeemable into coins, our nation's money has evolved into a fiat currency, irredeemable Federal Reserve notes and computer entries. Instead of a monetary system based on market principles, the Federal Reserve, a creation of the federal government, has a legal monopoly on creating "new" money, literally by the stroke of a computer key or a turn of the printing press.

The Fed's ability to create money puts it in a unique situation. It can buy assets (goods, services, or financial instruments) without first producing goods or services for the marketplace. The American people, on the other hand, must produce either in a factory or office and earn income (money) in order to obtain goods and services in the marketplace. The Fed, in other words, can obtain things without first producing. Sounds like a robber's activities and the Federal Reserve's are identical!

The Fed's power to create money has had an enormous impact on the U.S. economy since 1913. Since 1913, the dollar's purchasing power has declined by more than 95 percent. In addition, the U.S. economy has experienced the Great Depression and numerous mini-depressions, now called recessions. This is not a coincidence. The federal government's embrace of "monetary socialism" is directly responsible for the episodes of boom and bust the economy has experienced since the creation of the Federal Reserve.

Tax-Free 2000 explains how taxation, government spending, and monetary socialism have had—and are having—adverse effects on the people's standard of living. In addition, it offers a timetable to restructure the federal government as well as offering guidelines to deliver services to the people by both the profit and nonprofit sectors that are currently provided by state and local governments. Criticizing current policy is not a partisan political issue but a fundamentally philosophical one: What should the role of government be in a free society? An honest answer to this question would pave the way for a tax-free America.

Any society that does not implement a *laissez-faire* economic system will not operate at optimal efficiency nor produce the greatest output of goods and services. Think of the economy as a finely-tuned engine. The engine will operate smoothly as long as the fuel and air (the inputs) are properly mixed and not contaminated. The output (the horsepower) will be efficient at various engine speeds. An economy will produce the maximum amount of goods and services if manufacturers and employees are working together to meet consumer demands. Interfering with production (taxes, government spending, and regulations) will harm consumers as well as producers and employees. Moreover, an interventionist government will not nurture harmonious social relationships among the people. Taxation and government expenditures foment a continuous "civil war," because the spoils of taxation have to be divided among the country's "warring" factions. What criteria guide government officials in disbursing the people's money? Certainly not the criteria of the economic marketplace, which is violated when government takes the people's money in the form of taxes in the first place; instead, the "political" marketplace rules, where government panders to the people, dangling funds before them all in the name of compassion, concern, entitlement, or equity. This is the reality of the United States of America as the twentieth century draws to a close—a nation of "warriors" led by articulate, highly educated commanders, who have elevated "legal plunder" to the most sophisticated expression, the tax-and-spend policies of government.

The United States needs a radical, i.e., fundamental, prescription, for what ails the economy. Mere tinkering will only create more distortions undermining both the economy's ability to efficiently produce goods and services and the people's economic freedom and therefore postpone the "day of reckoning." Generations to come deserve a better legacy than what we will leave them if the statist quo, the belief in governmental solutions to most social and economic problems, is not overhauled. *Tax-Free 2000* is the only legacy that guarantees sustainable prosperity as well as the accomplishment of other noble goals—scientific, moral, cultural—that would inevitably flourish in a tax-free America.

1

Entering the Twentieth Century:

America's Counterrevolution Begins

> There was a time, long ago, when the average American could go about his daily business hardly aware of the government—especially the federal government. As a farmer, merchant, or manufacturer he could decide what, how, when, and where to produce and sell his goods, constrained by little more than market forces.
>
> --Robert Higgs

On December 31, 1899, the American people celebrated both the coming of a new year and a new century. For the 76 million Americans, memories of the nineteenth century were sometimes bitter, sometimes sweet. Some risked their lives to come to America with nothing but a hope and a prayer to build a better life for their families, and they did. Others may have believed the streets were paved with gold, and when they realized building a new life would not be easy, it is estimated that about one-third of the immigrants returned to their native lands. Yet, you could make a fortune in America . . . like Andrew Carnegie. Born in Scotland in 1835, he came to the United States as a boy with his family, worked in a cotton mill, became a telegraph operator, served as secretary to a manager of the Pennsylvania railroad, and eventually established an

iron works factory. His Pittsburgh steel company prospered
enormously in the post–Civil War expansion, and in 1901 he
sold his operations to J. P. Morgan for $480 million.

Clearly, not every immigrant became a Carnegie, but
America was known throughout the world as the land of
opportunity. Why else would millions of Europeans, Asians,
and people from other North and South American countries
flock to our shores in one of the greatest mass migrations the
world had ever seen? Immigration reached a nineteenth
century peak of nearly 800,000 in 1882, and no fewer than
125,000 came each year in the post–Civil War era (1865–
1900). Some came as skilled craftsmen, or professionals, but
the majority were unskilled or too young or too old to work.
They came for economic opportunity, but many also came for
liberty, the yearning to be free from the oppressive hand of the
state—the pogroms, the imprisonment, and the brutality of
their own governments.

Meanwhile, on the eve of the twentieth century, vivid
memories of the Civil War were still etched in people's minds.
With nearly 500,000 dead and the destruction of commerce,
industry and agriculture in the South, deep wounds were still
evident in sectional rivalry, threatening the great American
experiment in self-government and economic freedom. Despite the brutality of the 1860s, the republic survived and
slavery was eliminated, but the economic, political, and social
consequences of the War between the States were to have far-
reaching impacts, as we will discuss later.

For still others, life, even without war, was hard. In
1874, a young Minnesota farm girl wrote the state's governor
describing her family's lack of food, little clothing, and
meager bedding. In addition, their farmhouse was unbearably
cold because they didn't have the money to buy the lime
needed to make to plaster walls. She asked that he send money.
In 1894, during the depression of the nineties, a Kansas

housewife wrote her state's governor explaining that she is starving in "this God forsaken country." By 3 o'clock that day she still hadn't had anything to eat.[1]

Although these are heart-wrenching episodes—and undoubtedly there were countless others, especially in the slums of the nations' biggest cities where sanitary conditions were sometimes abominable—the United States completed its first full century as one of the world's greatest agricultural producers and industrial giants. Progress did not benefit every American immediately in the nineteenth century, nor has poverty been eliminated a century later in our nearly $6 trillion economy either. But, the economic data reveal the enormous output of goods and services that transformed the United States from a rebellious agricultural colony at the end of the eighteenth century to a fledgling independent nation within a decade to an economic powerhouse in a century. This was one of history's greatest achievements.

While generation after generation of Americans in general have prospered since its founding, some observers have suggested that free-market capitalism—*laissez-faire*—is responsible for the poverty and deprivation that has afflicted millions of families throughout American history. Their incontrovertible proof: America is a free enterprise society, poverty existed and still exists, therefore the free market causes poverty. This chain of "reasoning" is at best faulty, at worst it is the "Big Lie." As we shall see, only the free market generates prosperity. Government intervention benefits some people at the expense of the many in society. Proponents of *statism*—the misguided idea that government (spending and regulation) creates wealth—believe if only the federal government or the states and cities would spend more, poverty would be alleviated.

The fact that poverty exists and was evident throughout American history is not an indictment of free enterprise. On the contrary, prosperity increased and spread through society when government's involvement in the economy was limited. Moreover, poverty is a "natural" phenomenon. In other words, take any group of people from the industrialized world and drop them off on a remote island or in a tropical jungle, their standard of living will be incredibly low— guaranteed. In short, they will be living in poverty. Poverty is eradicated essentially through one process—capital formation. The creation and application of tools to improve living standards is the only process to eliminate poverty in the long run for the general population. That poverty exists among abundance is explicable because some families' breadwinner or breadwinners suffer from illness, accident, disability, or other unfortunate situations. In addition, if the head of the household lacks marketable skills, the family will have a low standard of living. And, when families found themselves in these unfortunate circumstances, the American tradition of community assistance operated, whether through religious groups, ethnic associations, trade organizations, or other voluntary means. Finally, there is a growing body of literature indicating that the government's welfare policies, employment regulations, and other well-intentioned efforts to reduce poverty have actually increased poverty in America.

The evidence indicates that the children and grandchildren and descendants of the immigrant and native "poor" of the nineteenth century and early twentieth century become doctors, lawyers, entrepreneurs, engineers, scientists, judges, professors, entertainers, professional athletes, and yes, even public officials—presidents, senators, governors, and mayors. With such a historical record of achievement, one would think that the nation's nineteenth century economic system would be untouched. Yet, the great irony of the post-Civil War era is that while the nation's economic performance was breathtaking, the call from both respectable intellectual quarters and some political figures for substantial government participation in the economy continued unabated.

While the proponents of relative *laissez-faire* won most of the political battles in the late nineteenth century to keep government's role in the economy limited, by the early twentieth century the great transformation accelerated and culminated in the ratification of the Sixteenth Amendment in February 1913 and the signing of the Federal Reserve Act by President Wilson in December of that year. By 1913, the major transformation of the U.S. economy was virtually completed; further encroachments were made by the federal government during the New Deal of the 1930s and the Great Society of the 1960s and 1970s. These interventions were made possible by the policies enacted through the early twentieth century. But, 1913 was the watershed year, transforming the economy from a relatively *laissez-faire* system to a quasi-socialized, semi-free enterprise system. In short, the federal government was transformed from Lilliputian to leviathan.

Why did it happen? How did it happen? What are the consequences for the American people as we enter the twenty-first century, if "leviathan" grows?

Before we tackle these questions, we need to know: What happened in the nineteenth century and early twentieth century that prompted the American people to accept the great transformation? Were they aware that a major transformation was occurring? Did they understand the consequences of further intervention? An overview of the U.S. economy will uncover what apparently went wrong with the American experiment in self-government and economic freedom that paved the way for semi-socialism in America.

America's Booming Century: Prosperity and Critics

America in the Nineteenth Century

Twenty-four years after declaring independence from Great Britain, the newly established United States had a population of 5.3 million people spread over nearly 900,000 square miles. The overwhelming proportion of Americans lived in rural areas (4.99 million), while only 322,000 lived in areas classified as urban. No one lived in an urban place with more than 100,000 people. A century later, the country more than tripled in size (2.97 million square miles), the population skyrocketed to 76.1 million citizens, with 30.1 million Americans living in urban areas and 45.8 million living in rural locations. Now, thirty-eight cities had populations over 100,000 including three cities with at least one million inhabitants. The urbanization of America occurred at a feverish pace. America's urban cities became meccas for Italians, Poles, Russians, Jews, and others who settled in the eastern ports and industrial cities of the Midwest. Many Germans and Scandinavians settled in farming communities of the upper Midwest as well as the bustling urban centers. Economic opportunity was one of the prime motivators for settling in places where industry, commerce, finance, transportation, etc., thrived. Even if the adult immigrants could only find menial work here, they believed their children would grow up as English-speaking Americans and would have the opportunity to become professionals or business executives.

Although economic data prior to the Civil War is sketchy at best, there are more reliable data about the U.S. economy's performance during the postwar period. The agricultural sector was the economy's foundation for much of the nineteenth century, and the growth of the population both here and abroad meant many mouths to feed and bodies to clothe (from cotton and wool). Between 1839 and 1899, farm income nearly quintupled in current prices, $713 million to $3.45 billion. Real farm income (in 1879 prices) amazingly quintupled too, from $787 million in 1839 to $4.02 billion in 1899. The number of agricultural workers rose from 1.4 million in 1800 to 11.7 million in 1900. Monthly wage rates with room and board increased from ten dollars in 1866 to fourteen dollars in 1899. At first glance, it appears farm laborers during the last third of the century did not enjoy the benefits of the booming economy, but prices were falling throughout this period. According to one available set of price data, consumer prices in 1899 were approximately 50 percent lower than in 1866. (Other indices indicate the cost of living dropping between 20 and 40 percent.) If we accept the greater price decline data, a 40 percent nominal wage hike is, in effect, nearly a threefold real wage hike! Who says deflation— falling prices—is harmful to the working class?

Farm productivity soared during the nineteenth century. In 1800, it took 373 man-hours per 100 bushels to harvest wheat, but only 106 man-hours in 1900. By 1900, cotton output was double the 1870 level and tobacco production was nearly three times greater than thirty years earlier. The output of meat, vegetables, and dairy products more than tripled between 1870 and 1900. Prices received by farmers, however, were dropping, reflecting the general price deflation throughout the 1800s as well as the substantial increase in the number of farms and acreage cultivated. In addition, farmers were able to increase production because of the great investment made in agricultural machinery and the spread of railroads, which made shipping goods from farmers to urban markets more efficient, especially over long distances.

If agricultural workers' incomes did exceedingly well over the century, especially during the latter one-third, and if farmers in general had rising incomes despite falling prices, how well did manufacturing workers and other laborers fare?

On the eve of the Civil War (1860), the labor force was 11.1 million, with 5.9 million persons engaged in agriculture, 1.5 million employed in manufacturing, and 890,000 employed in trade. By 1900, the U.S. labor force jumped to 29.1 million. Agricultural workers doubled in number (11.17 million), and manufacturing workers nearly quadrupled (5.9 million). Workers in trade more than quadrupled (4.0 million). The number of railway workers increased dramatically from 80,000 to 1 million in four decades, while the number of construction workers more than tripled (530,000 to 1.7 million). Rounding out the dramatic shift in the economy's dependence from agriculture to industry, the number of workers in the mining sector rose from 176,000 to 637,000. Thus, the proportion of agricultural workers in the economy declined from just under 50 percent in 1860 to 36 percent in 1900 as the industrial expansion accelerated in the latter part of the century.

Real average annual earnings of nonfarm employees rose from $332 in 1866 to $573 in 1900, 78 percent increase. Real earnings had plunged from 1860 to 1866 because of the Civil War inflation, so 1866 was the first full year of peace and the adjustments to a civilian economy as the appropriate base. However, in 1860, real average annual earnings were $457, a level that would not be reached until 1883. The Civil War apparently caused a major setback in the average American worker's income growth for more than twenty years. The costs of war had evidently more consequences than the death and destruction that occurred during the 1860s; the war undermined the natural progress that was initiated with the rapid industrialization of the U.S. economy.

The growth in real incomes of workers in the industrial sector during the 1800s is no surprise. The U.S. economy was pouring out producers' goods—steel, iron, chemicals, farm equipment, machinery, fabricated metals, locomotives, office equipment, construction equipment—at a rate that led to the doubling of real per capita gross national product (GNP) between 1870 and 1900. Private gross construction more than tripled in real terms between 1869 and 1873 and from 1897–1901, from $7.0 billion annual average in the former period to $26.7 billion in the latter period.

The American economy was on the move. No obstacle seemed insurmountable. Robert Higgs observed, "On the eve of the Great War Americans consumed about three times more economic goods per capita than they had a half century earlier. They lived longer and healthier lives and spent less time at work and more at recreation. They were better housed and educated, traveled more, read more, and were better informed about their own and other countries."[2]

But, the late nineteenth and early twentieth centuries were times of great social, financial, economic, and political stress. The identification of the stress points in American society will reveal why the great transformation of the United States occurred when it appeared that progress and innovation of the post-Civil War era seemed unstoppable, and optimism filled the air in spite of the hard times fared by some farming families, and newly arrived immigrants. With positive economic developments unfolding throughout the 1865–1900 period, there was, however, an undercurrent of discontent, which was manifested in political movements, and in popular books and numerous articles. Why discontent should emerge within the U.S. population w.   economy experienced one of the greatest booms in its history is at first glance an anomaly, but becomes crystal clear when the facts are examined.

Several major issues dominated U.S. political debates in the post-Civil War era—money and banking, the protective tariff, and the concentration of business. All three dominated political discussion, and the resolution of these issues in effect laid the foundation for the great transformation of 1913—the federal income tax and the Federal Reserve Act.

In retrospect, an inkling of the great transformation of 1913 occurred during the Civil War. During the war, the federal government introduced irredeemable fiat currency, the so-called greenbacks, to pay its bills, literally printing money, which was responsible for the price explosion from 1861-1865. The Legal Tender Act of 1862 authorized the federal government to issue for all intents and purposes legalized counterfeit notes. These notes were not redeemable into gold, the money *par excellence* of the United States since its origin. The federal government resorted to the centuries-old method of obtaining resources to wage war, namely printing bits of paper to purchase goods and services in the marketplace, thereby causing price inflation. To wage a noninflationary war requires the government to either tax its citizens, thereby diverting purchasing power from the public to itself or tapping the public's savings by issuing debt securities. More often than not governments usually undertake all three methods, inflating, taxing, and borrowing, resulting in higher prices, lower real wages, lower productivity, and a higher national debt. Sound familiar? The Vietnam War experience of the 1960s and 1970s confirms how war and military expenditures had and are still having serious economic consequences for the U.S. economy.

During the Civil War, the federal government suspended the gold standard, thereby unleashing a price explosion. The federal government also enacted both the National Banking Acts (establishing a national banking system, which was a forerunner of the Federal Reserve System) and an income tax, which lasted until 1872. Suffice it to say, this centralized banking system destabilized the U.S. economy, causing the panics of 1873, 1884, 1893, and 1907. These financial crises unnerved the bankers, business interests, and the general public who wanted stability in their business affairs and personal lives, that is, more certainty in their daily affairs. Who could blame them? However, what they eventually agreed to, the Federal Reserve, replaced one destabilizing system with another.

Meanwhile, these crises were grist for the mill of paper money advocates, labor union leaders, Socialist party writers, and others who wanted more government involvement in the economy. And, here is the great irony. While the paper money system hampered economic growth after the Civil War (the greenbacks were the monetary standard until 1879 when gold convertibility was restored), productivity rose dramatically after the restoration of the gold standard. Yet, the alleged defects of gold-based money have been cited as the primary cause of U.S. economic fluctuations throughout this period. But, the evidence suggests otherwise. Fractional reserve banking, credit creation, and the silver agitation of the late nineteenth century intertwined to initiate the boom-bust cycle.

In the 1990s, as incredible as it may seem, we are experiencing the fallout of the Civil War money and banking question! In short, the money and banking question—arcane as it may be—is crucial to understanding the instability of the American economy as well as realizing why money became "socialized." Banking, in short, is one of the weakest economic links in our society and is undermining sustainable prosperity.

The Tariff Issue

The War of 1812, like previous and future hostilities, required enormous sums of money. To obtain the needed revenue, the federal government raised taxes, primarily custom duties on foreign goods, and also instituted new domestic taxes—"excise taxes on goods and commodities and taxes on houses, slaves and land."[3] After the war, the new taxes were eliminated and replaced by a high protective tariff in 1816, which was sufficient to retire the national debt by the mid 1830s.

Although the tariff issue became an important issue in the late 1820s after the passage of the 1828 tariff, the so-called Tariff of Abominations, which led South Carolina to protest and assert the *nullification doctrine*, the tariff would emerge as a national issue with far-reaching implications after the Civil War. For the period prior to the war, the tariff, from the southern states' perspective, was one of a long list of encroachments by the federal government on the region's economy. The tariff was favored by the manufacturing interests of the Northeast who did not want the cheap goods from overseas competing with its products. The South wanted freer trade so it could obtain less expensive machinery from abroad. Politically, this meant the Whigs, forerunners of the Republican party, were in favor of a high tariff inasmuch as their geographic base was in the Northeast. Democrats basically were in favor of low tariffs because they represented immigrants, small businessmen, and the working class of the South and West, in particular. In short, the lines were drawn for sectional/political rivalry that eventually led to the War Between the States. But, the South, unable to separate from the Union peacefully and forced to remain in the Union after the hostilities of 1861–1865, continued to engage in sectional rivalry with the Northeast after the war ended. But this was resolved peacefully as the great transformation took hold in 1913.

Meanwhile, during the Civil War, the North imposed higher tariffs to obtain revenue for the military effort against the South. Virtually no imported item was untouched by the tariff. The legacy of high tariffs was simple. The postwar economic boom filled the coffers of the U.S. Treasury for three decades, running substantial surpluses which were used to increase pensions for Civil War veterans and their families. Nevertheless, there was agitation to enact an income tax (68 bills were introduced to Congress between 1874 and 1894) by the Greenback Party, the Farmers' Alliance, and the Populists. Their thinking was straightforward: the tariff harmed low-income Americans, so replace this regressive levy with an income tax on the rich who had the ability to pay for running the government.

In 1887, President Grover Cleveland, a hard-money Democrat, wanted to lower tariffs because "he felt that the tariff should be for revenue only." In the 1888 presidential election, Cleveland lost the presidency even though he won the popular vote. In 1890, the new Republican administration of Benjamin Harrison signed the McKinley Tariff, which the Republican-controlled Congress had passed. Democrats, stunned by the dramatic rise in tariffs, took revenge at the polls in November 1890 and gained control of the House of Representatives. In the 1892 election, Grover Cleveland was re-elected to a nonconsecutive second term and the Democrats also took control of the Senate. The people spoke. Lower tariffs.

As Cleveland took office in 1893, the country's most severe depression of the century began, lasting until 1897. Times were hard. By some estimates, unemployment reached 30 percent in some states. Production plunged, strikes increased, violence erupted, and the federal budget surplus evaporated. The fabric of America was coming unravelled. An adviser to President Cleveland warned in 1894: "We are on the eve of a very dark night unless a return of commercial prosperity relieves popular discontent."[4]

In this environment, major reform is easier to accomplish—theoretically, at least. The Democrats believed the time was ripe to modify the McKinley Tariff and at the same time hold at bay the growing influence of Populists in the South and West. The Wilson-Gorman tariff bill (enacted by Congress on August 15, 1894, and named after the co-sponsors in the House and Senate, William L. Wilson and Arthur P. Gorman, respectively) reduced rates slightly and included an amendment authorizing an income tax. President Cleveland was unhappy with the provisions because it did not reduce tariffs enough and included a general income tax instead of "a few additional internal revenue taxes, including a small tax upon incomes derived from certain corporate investments."[5] Cleveland realized the government needed revenue to make up for the shortfalls that lower tariffs would cause, but he did not want nor advocate an income tax. He allowed the Wilson-Gorman bill to become law without his signature.

Again, sectional rivalries reared its head over the new law. The South and West felt the minimal reductions in tariffs still left the duties on imported goods burdensome to their sections of the country, while the Northeast benefited from the protection given to their industries.

In addition, the vote on the internal revenue provision of the bill also reflected this deep sectional split. In the House, 182 votes were cast in favor of the income tax, 177 of which were from the South and West. In the Senate, no senator from the Northeast voted in favor of the income tax. Suffice it to say, the income tax section of the tariff bill was declared unconstitutional in 1895. The Supreme Court in a 5–4 decision based its argument that the income-tax provision was a "direct" tax, and according to the Constitution, such taxes must be apportioned uniformly according to state population. Despite the Supreme Court's striking down of the income tax, this was a short-lived victory for the opponents of federal income taxation. During the next sixteen years, the income tax issue virtually disappeared from political discussion only to be resurrected in Congress in 1909. The next chapter will discuss the evolution of the income tax from a temporary measure to a permanent feature of the Constitution.

Big Business and the Age of the "Robber Barons"

The image of a post–Civil War businessman held by most Americans who have studied history can be summed up briefly: Greedy speculator gouging the public. This consensus view has been reinforced in public school textbooks, scholarly books and articles, and media discussions. But, as is often the case, along comes a marvelous, insightful book that explodes a widely held caricature; in this case venal entrepreneur preying on the poor and working classes.

In *The Myth of the Robber Barons*, history professor Burton W. Folsom, Jr., presents a comprehensive critique of the generally held view of the rise of Big Business in America, namely that it was a period of *laissez-faire* run amok and only the wise and necessary legislation enacted by the federal government prevented more abuses by corporate America. A detailed examination of the record suggests otherwise: that is, the abuses that occurred in the country were related to government intervention, not the free market.

According to Folsom, there were and are "political" entrepreneurs and "market" entrepreneurs. As Forrest McDonald explains in the Foreword to Folsom's book:

> The former were in fact comparable to medieval robber barons, for they sought and obtained wealth through the coercive power of the state, which is to say that they were subsidized by government and were sometimes granted monopoly status by government. Invariably, their products or services were inferior to and more expensive than the goods and services provided by market entrepreneurs, who sought and obtained wealth by producing more and better for less cost to the consumer. The market entrepreneurs, however, have been repeatedly—one is tempted to say systemically—ignored by historians. [6]

In his profile of Commodore Vanderbilt (steamships), James J. Hill (railroads), the Scrantons (iron works), Charles Schwab (steel), and John D. Rockefeller (oil), a common theme emerges. These businessmen either challenged existing government-created monopolies and offered better service at lower prices or had a better vision of America's industrial future and decided to participate in the enormous economic expansion of the post-Civil War era. In short, they were the quintessential risk takers, and they were rewarded handsomely in the free market for their skills and business foresight. Yet, scholars treat them as anti-social and "ruthless." Ruthless seems to be the favorite description of businessmen who lowered prices to consumers, thereby increasing the public's standard of living throughout the so-called robber baron age.

As Folsom shows, the criticism of the entrepreneurs who amassed great wealth is terribly misplaced. For without John D. Rockefeller's effort to build Standard Oil into the oil giant it became, the U.S. oil industry may never have developed because of the intense Russian competition. Rockefeller successfully waged a thirty-year battle with the Russians for a substantial share of the world market. "The spoils of victory— jobs, technology, cheap kerosene, cheap by-products, and cheap gas to spur the auto industry—all this might have been lost had it not been for Rockefeller's ability to sell oil profitably at six cents a gallon."[7] He was able to accomplish this Herculean task by eventually controlling 90 percent of U.S. refinery capacity by buying his competitors' facilities, sometimes at greatly inflated prices. By expanding judiciously and staying in business for the long haul instead of making a profit on short-term trading, as many oil entrepreneurs did, Rockefeller built an oil empire. But, since he was shipping great quantities of oil by rail, he was able to obtain discount rebates from Vanderbilt's New York Central. Protesting the rate "discrimination," other oil men were unhappy with both Rockefeller and Vanderbilt, even though the latter offered the same rates for anyone shipping the same volume of oil as Rockefeller. There were no takers because none was as efficient as Standard Oil. According to Folsom, Rockefeller made enemies. "Henry Demarest Lloyd, whose cousin was an unhappy oil man, wrote *Wealth Against Commonwealth* in 1894 to denounce Rockefeller. Ida Tarbell, whose father was a Pennsylvania oil producer, attacked Rockefeller in a series of articles for *McClure's* magazine."[8] Yet, Ida Tarbell, in a chapter entitled "The Legitimate Greatness of the Standard Oil Company" in *The History of the Standard Oil Company*, extols the company's organization, particularly the efficiency of its oil refining process.[9] So what's the concern? Was Standard Oil a good corporate citizen or a fledgling monopoly that crushed competitors unmercifully?

The petroleum industry began in 1859 when oil was found in Titusville, Pennsylvania. From its chaotic beginnings—prices fluctuating wildly, oil and its derivatives being dumped anywhere—the industry grew spectacularly in the post-Civil War era. However, during the 1870s, as prices fell markedly because of the federal government's deflationary policies (which were instituted to restore the gold standard in 1879) only efficient industrial firms were able to survive. The number of oil refineries declined, and by 1880 "John D. Rockefeller was the undisputed king of petroleum."[10]

In 1882, the Standard Oil Trust was formed in order to efficiently manage the fourteen companies Standard Oil controlled and the stock it owned in approximately twenty-five other firms. The trust, in effect, was a holding company for the stockholders of the thirty-nine companies associated with Standard. The stockholders surrendered their stock to nine trustees and received trust certificates for the shares tendered. For ten years, the trust operated without interference, until March 1892 when the Ohio Supreme Court ordered Standard Oil of Ohio to withdraw from the arrangement because it ruled the trust was illegal. Standard Oil of New Jersey was then organized as a legal holding company in 1899.

From the late 1890s until the Standard Oil Trust was dissolved, the oil industry changed dramatically. New supplies flowed from Kansas, Oklahoma, Texas, and California and new integrated companies were formed. Standard Oil kept growing but its market share was dwindling markedly, down to 11 percent in 1906 from 34 percent in 1898 and to 20 percent in 1902. Moreover, the "share of the petroleum products market fell from approximately 88 percent in 1890, to 68 percent in 1907, and then 64 percent in 1911." As one analyst concluded, "To seriously maintain that Standard was increasingly monopolizing the petroleum industry at the turn of the century, or that the antitrust suit against Standard, begun in 1906, was a legitimate response to almost complete monopolistic control, is patently absurd."[11]

With the print media publishing anti-big business articles and several best-selling popular books expressing critical views of large corporations *per se* even if they were efficient, created jobs, and were instrumental in the nation's economic development, the environment was not hospitable for the courts to render any decision affirming corporations the right to organize in a manner perceived to be anti-competitive. In late 1909, Standard was convicted of violating the antitrust laws; the Supreme Court upheld the lower court's decision in May 1911.

After a thorough review of the Supreme Court's decision, economics professor D. T. Armentano concluded that the Court engaged in faulty reasoning in upholding the antitrust suit against Standard Oil. Armentano takes the Court to task for citing Standard Oil's growth as proof that it wanted to monopolize and thereby restrain trade in the petroleum industry. But as we saw above, Standard Oil's market share within the industry was declining rapidly because of the new oil fields and new competitors. Thus, the Supreme Court engaged in legal gymnastics to uphold the conviction of Standard Oil, not because it was harming the public, but because it was too efficient. In the final analysis, politics played an important element in the government's pursuit of Standard Oil. As Gabriel Kolko points out in his analysis of the progressive period, President Theodore Roosevelt believed there were "good" trusts and "bad" trusts. Standard Oil was deemed a bad trust, and hence the rigorous pursuit of antitrust violations against the company. Meanwhile, large corporations allied with the House of Morgan, the epitome of Wall Street capital, were generally treated with a hands-off attitude.[12]

What can we make of these developments? Clearly, there were no definitive principles guiding public officials because the Sherman Anti trust Act of 1890 was so nebulous regarding "monopoly" or "intent" to monopolize, "restraint of trade," and "predatory" pricing. A much broader question, however, emerged. What is the proper role of government in the economy and how to deal with the evolving corporate sector?

Railroads and Regulation

Probably in no other sector of the economy during the post–Civil War era were the lines as clearly drawn between political entrepreneurship and market entrepreneurship than in the railroad industry. This should not come as a surprise to students of history given the massive federal government subsidies, including loans and land grants, some railroads received. Not coincidentally, the two most subsidized systems, the Union Pacific and Central Pacific, built their respective lines quickly and shoddily—because the more they built the greater the subsidies they received. It has been estimated that the Union Pacific was so inefficient that construction costs were three times what they should have been. In 1869, the two railroads joined in Utah with America's first transcontinental railroad. (Actually, the Union Pacific started in Omaha and the Central Pacific in Sacramento.) Despite the hoopla "both of the shoddily constructed lines had to be rebuilt and sometimes relocated, a task that the UP didn't finish until five years later." America's first federal government involvement in railroad expansion was by all accounts a fiasco. Eventually UP went bankrupt in 1893, while the Central Pacific became a mo-

nopoly in the truest sense of the word, outlawing competition
in California and prospering because of its exalted status. Its
shady dealings were chronicled by Frank Norris in the novel,
The Octopus.[13]

The federal government subsidized another railroad,
the Northern Pacific, through the country's northwest region
not with loans but land grants in the late 1860s. Unsuccessful,
the railroad nevertheless continued operation, even going
through a bankruptcy, before Henry Villard gained control in
1881. A wheeler-dealer, Villard thought the Northwest would
be an ideal resort area and developed some health spas in
Montana. The spas went under. Villard failed because he
expanded the railroad to gain federal subsidies, not to accommodate market demand for transportation in the sparsely
populated region. In short, the federal government's role in
America's economic development should have been an em-
barrassment to government officials. Instead of ending the
subsidization of railroads, the federal government and the
states poured $350 million of taxpayers' money into the
industry, not including the land grants.[14]

When a new industry develops, the market, that is, free
enterprise can be counted on to develop and market the
product or service and expand if conditions warrant. Or
governments, too, may get involved for a variety of reasons,
e.g., the prestige of having the good or service expand rapidly
and hence obtain more tax revenues, and "safeguard" the
public welfare by promulgating guidelines on the types of
services to offer and prices to charge customers. In addition,
entrepreneurs may seek subsidies in order to reduce or eliminate their risks inherent in an untested marketplace. By
cajoling, persuading, or bribing legislators, subsidies can give
a boost—an artificial one—to a fledgling company or industry. This appears to have been the case in the development of
the railroad industry in the United States. In other words,
political entrepreneurship dominated the railroads.

Unlike many political entrepreneurs, James J. Hill built the Great Northern Line in the northwest region without government aid and where the Northern Pacific had failed. Hill's achievement is all the more remarkable when you consider he bought a defunct line, the St. Paul and Pacific Railroad, and completed it slowly through the Northwest, assisting the local farm economy so farmers would have products to ship on his railroad. Instead of relying on government subsidies—in effect a "take the money and run" scheme when it came to the railroads—Hill helped create viable economies so his railroad would be an integral element—the infrastructure in today's lingo of a prosperous, developing region. And, according to Albro Martin, author of *James J. Hill and the Opening Up of the Northwest*, Hill's vision, providing railroad service "to nearly every village and town of consequence . . . changed the character of American life forever."[15]

Even when the economy suffered a depression, such as the downturn that began in 1893, Hill, true to his entrepreneurial spirit, wrote to a railroad owner who was one of many lobbying the federal government for loans. "The government should not furnish capital to these companies, in addition to their enormous land subsidies, to enable them to conduct their business in competition with enterprises that have received no aid from the public Treasury."[16] Hill clearly delineated the difference between "fair" and "unfair" competition—risking capital in the marketplace and feeding at the public trough. The gross inefficiencies of the subsidized railroads, therefore, aroused the public against them and culminated in the creation of the Interstate Commerce Commission in 1887, the Sherman Antitrust Act (1890) and the Hepburn Act (1906).[17] In short, free enterprise did not fail, but government subsidies led to more government intervention, punishing the Hills of the nation.

However, the increase in government regulation was, according to Gabriel Kolko in his insightful *Railroads and Regulation:1877—1916,* not unwelcomed by railroad interests, who saw national regulation as a means to override the "cumbersome and unpredictable" state regulations being enacted. In addition, the railroad men sought to have the regulators exert a semblance of stability in their fragmented and competitive industry. One way to accomplish this "rationalization" of the industry was to prevent rebates and thus increase revenues, and second, under the guise of reform, prop up rates while appearing to be upholding the public interest against the railroads.

Although Kolko presents convincing evidence that railroad entrepreneurs lobbied and even welcomed federal regulation, the reasons varied. If federal regulations were seen as less cumbersome than the multitude of state regulations, some railroad executives may have seen the federal government as the lesser of two evils, dealing with one "devil" rather than several dozen. On the other hand, self-interest may have been the overriding concern for the railroad magnates, namely, beating the competition using the political means—government—instead of outcompeting them in the marketplace. If competitors can make profits with lower rates, inefficient railroads will be driven out of business. But, if railroads must charge the same rate as the inefficient entrepreneurs, then the government has interceded in the marketplace and harmed shippers and consumers, and kept the political entrepreneurs operating when the free market wanted them out of business. As Kolko reveals, the voluntary cartel of railroads did not work, so some of the railroad operators turned to the only agency in society then can legally mandate a cartel, the government.[18]

Summary

In addition to the political railroad entrepreneurs ideological factors played a role in expanding government regulation of the railroads, particularly that of the economy in general. The enormous upheaval of American society in the last third of the nineteenth century was unsettling to the American people. After the Civil War, Americans wanted stability, certainty, and most of all, peace and prosperity. They obtained the latter, but clearly unevenly throughout the century, as immigration, urban growth, industrial expansion, and labor unrest put substantial strains on the people. And, people reacted differently whether in the nativist movement, the labor union movement, religious revivalism, or dabbling in utopian schemes such as socialism.

The political mechanism absorbed, digested, and formulated policies to correct perceived or real grievances. But, as the nineteenth century drew to a close, the Panic of 1893 and the ensuing depression left an indelible mark on the nation. The Panic began after gold exports increased in 1892 thereby making the U. S. dollar less trustworthy. The fractional-reserve banking system could not handle the bank runs that were occurring. With the stock market crash in the spring of 1893, the financial house of cards collapsed.[19] The American century was drawing to an end and the people were unsure whether sustainable prosperity could ever be achieved. What could be done? The monetary instability of the 1890s was corrected as the century drew to a close, prosperity resumed, and the new century began on a hopeful note. By the time the Panic of 1907 occurred, the nation's ideological shift, especially among major opinion molders, was virtually completed. As Robert Higgs sums up the era:

> The big meat packers who pushed for the Meat Inspection
> Act, the shippers who fought for amendments to the Interstate
> Commerce Act, the proponents of trustbusting and the Trade

Commission and the income tax amendment—all shared a willingness, often an eagerness to expand the scope of effective governmental authority over economic decision-making.

...Notwithstanding the gradual tendency toward intervention-ism at the state and local levels in the late nineteenth century, the dominant ideology of the 1890s—the one embraced by the majority of opinion leaders, government officials, and (so far as one can judge) most of the public as well—held that government, especially the federal government, had only a limited mission... After 1900, virtually all important public-policy proposals called for more extensive governmental ac-tion, particularly for more extensive action by the federal government.[20]

This ideological shift that Higgs refers to can be traced to multiple causes, the social and economic transformation of the U.S. society, the belief that *laissez-faire* was responsible for harming the public's welfare, and the economic instability which was precipitated by the federal government's monetary manipulations, all contributed to setting the stage for America's 1913 counterrevolution, the passage of the Sixteenth Amend-ment, constitutionally guaranteeing a federal income tax and the enactment of the Federal Reserve Act.

We will examine these two institutions in order to shed light on America's evolution from a relatively *laissez-faire* economy to a quasi-socialistic nation.

2

The Income Tax:

Organized Plunder or Necessary Evil?

Robbery differs from taxation in that it is a one-time operation.

--H. S. Ferns

Taxes are the price we pay for civilized society.

--Oliver Wendell Holmes, Jr.

Everyone can name the world's oldest profession, but how many people know what is probably the world's second oldest profession? Sad, but true, the tax collector. He may have first appeared as far back as 3000 B.C. Not surprisingly, the world's oldest two professions have more in common than just longevity. In Mesopotamia, the cradle of civilization, monarchs received income from temple prostitutes.[1] (Does this mean that pimping is the world's third oldest profession?) That prostitution and taxation have been interrelated should not be shocking. Both obtain money using morally questionable acts. If prostitution is an immoral selling of one's body, then taxation can be described as a continuous form of robbery, that is, the taking of the people's money without their consent. Both practices are alive and well after five thousand years; taxation still is entrenched virtually everywhere, and prostitution is generally considered unacceptable social behavior; nevertheless, it is legal in some locations throughout the world, including parts of Nevada.

Enough about prostitution, although it has a fascinating history. Needless to say, the emphasis in this chapter is to review how income and other taxes grew and grew and grew. For if the proponents of tax and spend, or tax, borrow and spend are confident their (interventionist) policies are best for the economy, then logically they should advocate total and complete socialism—100 percent taxation!—so the state could have complete control over society's resources and thus be able to allocate them according to the ruling elite's vision of how to promote jobs and prosperity. Economists and other academics and public officials who believe in a government-assisted, government-subsidized, government-directed economy, should embrace the logic of their position, namely, that socialism will increase the public's standard of living better than *laissez-faire*. If they are unwilling to embrace full socialism, then they have to explain how semi-socialism will serve the people better than *laissez-faire*.

The purpose of this chapter is to demonstrate that Frank Chodorov's assertion that not only is the income tax the "root of all evil,"[2] but that all taxes are hazardous to the people's general well being.

The Taxman Cometh

The Ancient World

In ancient Egypt, taxes were levied on the production of grain, vineyards, fruit, fish, honey, etc. Although they were not "direct" income taxes, each levy "was simply an income tax without much sophistication," because it was a tax on gross production.[3] Rates in the ancient world varied from one-sixth to one-fourth, but occasionally reached one-half. In a world where a subsistence existence was the rule rather than the exception, any tax beyond a mere pittance was, as you could imagine, onerous.

Examining the ancient world reveals an underlying theme in the history of taxation. Empire building is the prevalent practice of kings, monarchs, dictators and, as we shall see, modern nation-states. To build an empire requires a large military to conquer lands in order to enrich the state. In many instances, laborers served as soldiers. In fact, "in the ancient Egyptian language the word *labor* was a synonym for taxes."[4] In other civilizations, men gave "a specified number of days of labor to the priest-king." And, in conquered territories a bureaucracy to administer both the peoples and their wealth was required so that resources could flow to the victorious state. In short, taxation was implemented to prepare for war, was increased to fight the battles, and was spread to the conquered areas. War, as one modern analyst observed, is the health of the state. Taxation then was and is the tonic to enlarge and expand the state at the expense of the people who do the dying, provide the foodstuffs and materials, and, in a money economy, the coins or other forms of money to purchase the armaments.

But, taxation had other effects besides transferring (no confiscating!) the people's wealth for the benefit of the state. As Charles Adams states:

> The tax story of ancient Egypt shows what happens in a society burdened with a totalitarian revenue system. The informer, the corrupt revenue official and—most significantly—the tyranny of all pervading surveillance are inherent in such a system. Every taxable transaction must be recorded and subject to examination. Consequently, the individual has to submit every aspect of his life to tax inquisition.[5]

Sound familiar? Americans who file 1040s and have been audited by the IRS realize that individuals charged with murder, rape, and armed robbery appear to have more legal protection than law-abiding citizens who become embroiled in tax disputes with the federal government.

In the ancient world, recalcitrant citizens were physically abused by tax collectors. Sometimes, taxes were forgiven. However, when tax evasion reached levels that threatened the state's power, heads of state would send in troops to subdue the populace so they would comply with the tax edicts. Occasionally, rebellion would break out. The evidence suggests that rebellions occurred frequently because "the burden of supporting government in highly stratified, agriculturally based societies of the ancient world fell disproportionately upon the poor, "as well as 'an unpopular' wealthy class, without political power," such as the Jews in Egypt and the Jewish population of the Kingdom of Israel.[6] When the Assyrians demanded taxes and were challenged by the kingdom's population, the Jews were no match for the Assyrians who systematically crushed them. Eventually, the Assyrians were replaced by the Babylonians as the power in the region and were just, if not more, tyrannical in both imposing and collecting taxes, such as the taking of the eyes of Zedekiah, king of Judah, by Nebuchadnezzar, king of Babylon.

In the final analysis, "as far as the ordinary person was concerned, all ancient regions were despotisms."[7] With fairly strict hierarchical structures in place, the common man eked out his life, hoping to reach age 20 or 30, the life expectancy of most people. Not being able to attain a different social class from which he was born, and living under the yoke of a pharaoh, king, or emperor, the common man of 3,000–5,000 years ago was, to say the least, heavily taxed by any standard. Even if direct taxes were relatively low, the indirect taxes consisting of labor service rendered to the state, and the levies on goods, effectively made near-slaves of much of the population.

As we move on to Greece, the birthplace of Western civilization, the issue of taxation takes on a rather unique phase. To the Greeks, direct taxation represented tyranny. Thus, indirect taxation was considered a safeguard against a tyrannical state. What taxes did exist were relatively low and levied on various commercial activities, e.g., sales, imports, etc. Other taxes were imposed on users of such public facilities as roads, bridges, sea lanes, or harbors. In short, these taxes were, in effect, user fees which covered the costs of operating the facilities. Moreover, foreigners, in the final analysis, paid the substantial bulk of taxes in Athens because they gathered there to engage in the hustle and bustle of the city's economic life. Charles Adams sums up why Greece became successful.

> ... good laws protecting property, sound money, safe sea lanes and low taxes were the foundation of Greek prosperity and liberty.[8]

Nevertheless, some city-states were ruled by tyrants who imposed direct taxes. Assassination of tyrants was justified because tyranny, in the form of direct taxation, was unacceptable to the Greeks. However, they occasionally imposed direct taxes on foreigners, who paid a monthly poll tax, a *metoikion*, "one drachma for men and a half a drachma for women." A drachma was the Greek silver coin that provided a stable currency for the population, and hence was an essential element of Greek prosperity.

For the most part, average Athenians did not pay taxes. Instead of relying on the coercive powers of the state to obtain funds for public facilities, the Greek employed a fascinating method known as *liturgy*. The liturgy was simply donations by wealthy citizens to maintain public facilities such as bridges, gymnasia, etc., to fund the costs of religious festivals held periodically during the year and provide military equipment for defense of the state. This voluntary payment may seem strange to us, but it functioned successfully because of "tradition and strong public sentiment."[9] Wealthy citizens were expected to support the community with their contributions, and they did. In fact, "wealthy citizens tried to draw public attention to their generosity." Also, in times of emergency to combat aggressors, "extraordinary" liturgies were implemented, which became more or less permanent for approximately two centuries. Eventually, these liturgies were replaced by the *eisphora*, a tax on capital assets of the wealthy, which provided the revenue for equipping the naval forces. The eisphora was self-administered. The wealthy citizens were divided into groups in which they made declarations of their wealth. The groups were led by a president and two vice presidents who had to pay the entire assessment immediately. They, in turn, would have to collect from the other members the appropriate assessment. Needless to say, each group's triumvirate had a strong motivation to collect as soon as possible. Because it was a direct tax, it was considered a form of tyranny, thus the tax was strictly for emergency measures and then canceled when hostilities cleared. Moreover, when the spoils of war were obtained, they would be "used to repay or refund the eisphora."[10]

From our perspective, two thousand years later, how should we view the liturgy to fund public revenues? According to Charles Adams:

> . . . the liturgy was the device by which the Greeks achieved civilization without despotism. When a government takes wealth by force and claim of right, it is inclined to trample on the people's property rights and liberties. On the other hand, if private wealth is spend *(sic)* without social conscience on the extravagances of individuals, the less fortunate suffer and are often driven to violence and revolution. The liturgy was a solution to the dilemma of too much versus too little government intervention in the accumulation of private property. The

interests of the community and the individual were reasonably
balanced. The liturgy respected private property, but it also
induced the wealthy to shoulder the main burden of providing
for the needs of the community—and the genius of the system
lay in the fact that no police power was needed to achieve those
ends.[11]

Unrepentant "liberals" would recoil at the prospect of
eliminating "progressive" taxation because in ancient Greece
the wealthy financed eventually all the construction of public
facilities—roads, buildings, etc. Fees were assessed as was
mentioned earlier to pay for the upkeep, which makes eminent
sense. But, since the Greeks were building a civilization from
square one, the liturgy may have been more appropriate for
them. Trying to replace our system with the liturgy may be
difficult, but not impossible.

In addition to the liturgy, the Greeks invented tax
farming, the hiring of private contractors to collect taxes. Tax
farming is a bizarre form of "free enterprise." Although tax
farming was more efficient "than the direct government tax
collection practices, the people came to fear the tax farmers for
their abuses and oppressive tactics." In a way, this was a
brilliant strategy of the government because it deflected opposition from public officials to the wealthy individuals who
were the only ones capable of undertaking this task. Tax
farmers not only collected taxes, but loaned money to individuals to pay their taxes, thus serving as bankers to hapless
taxpayers. Their other activities included wholesaling the
farmer's products which they taxed, as well as brokering grain
and wine.[12]

Another important lesson from Greece deals with the
budget. If the budget was unbalanced, reduction in expenditures was considered the most prudent method to get the
Kingdom's financial affairs in order.[13] In short, the Greeks
were savvy financial and social analysts and understood the
importance of moderate fiscal policies for prosperity and
social stability.

The Greek legacy of taxation has been virtually abandoned in the Western world; keep taxes indirect and low and
establish a sense of community so that all citizens, including
the poor, would voluntarily pay for public facilities and
services. In its place, modern governments have resorted to
coercion and compulsion—methods that undermine the
public's trust in the government, breeding fear, distrust, and
opposition. When the coercion and oppression reached intolerable levels, rebellion usually occurred. Although "the Greek
ideals about taxation were short-lived in Greece . . . the
Romans forbade direct taxation of its citizens for almost 500
years."[14] Still the Roman Empire collapsed, not for a lack of
taxation but because of the inherent flaws of state aggrandize-
ment.

The collapse of the Roman Empire in 476 A.D., when
Rome was seized by King Odovacar, was the culmination of
abandoning several hundred years of relatively sound tax and
economic policies and replacing them with the totalitarianism
of Diocletian, who imposed every interventionist, socialistic
policy from debasing the currency, increasing taxes, and
imposing direct taxes to nationalizing commerce. During
Diocletian's reign (284–305 A.D.), price inflation skyrocketed,
price controls were enforced by penalty of death, and the
number of tax agents swelled to collect revenue for the state.
The logical consequences of the economic and social instability that gripped the empire, however, would not be fully felt for
more than a hundred years.

With taxes so burdensome, tax evasion rose dramatically, making it difficult to have sufficient revenue to protect
Rome from invaders. Could this be the immediate cause of
Rome's fall—tax evasion?[15] In short, did Rome collapse
because of the statist policies Diocletian and his successors set
into motion, thus undermining society's relationships which
are essential for sustainable prosperity? If so, there is a lesson
here for the U.S. experience of the past eighty years.

Throughout the early Roman Republic's history, taxation was modest by their standards, a 2 percent customs duty in Spain, while "in Sicily, Africa and Albania the rate was 5 percent."[16] Slaves were taxed at auction, in port by customs, and when they were sold; the rates varied from 2-5 percent. In conquered colonies, existing taxes on land and product were maintained but not increased. Voluntary service of the citizenry was also a way of funding state activities in lieu of monetary payments. As the Roman Empire expanded, gold and silver flowed to Rome from Spain forming the basis of its monetary system for the next several centuries.[17]

In the second century B.C., a form of state capitalism developed. Businessmen became brutal and oppressive tax farmers in the conquered territories, and soon they were able to dominate the commercial activities of Rome with the income they received from their tax-collecting activities.[18] Because they—the *publicans*—effectively funded the Roman government, they wielded enormous power and influence. Eventually, the publicans lost their power after they banded together to eliminate Rhodes as a commercial rival in the region. With the decline of Rhodian activity, the seas became more dangerous to Roman shipping because Rhodes's naval power had made the high seas safe for commerce. In 88 B.C., meanwhile, an anti-tax rebellion in what is now Turkey killed 80,000 Roman publicans and another "20,000 Romans and pro-Roman Greek businessmen were slaughtered at the freeport of Delos." (The numbers may have been overstated.) General Sulla crushed the revolt and ordered prepayment of five years' taxes as well as the cost of his four-year military campaign. To enforce his decree, "special agents" were created who had the power to collect the tax and behead any tax resister.[19] The collection of taxes now literally involved "your money or your life." Eventually, the Roman Senate in turn empowered General Pompey to crush the pirates plundering the ships.

When Julius Caesar took over the reins of power, he believed taxes should be lowered in order to gain the loyalty of Rome's provinces. When the harvest was poor, taxes were renegotiated. The murder of Caesar overturned the peaceful relations Rome enjoyed with the eastern provinces. Brutus and his successor Mark Antony looted and plundered as much as they could. When the civil wars ended, Octavian reduced taxes and eliminated the last vestiges of the publicans.[20]

The ascension of Caesar Augustus (30 B.C.) ushered in an era of relative peace and stability, the foundation for a two-hundred year period of prosperity. In 60 A.D., however, a revolt in England against the Roman administration led to the death of 70,000 people in London. The Roman Empire's brutality on several occasions cannot be condoned in any shape, way or form. The lesson is that empire building is destructive of human life and property. During his rule, he reduced the power of the Senate by effectively decentralizing tax collections so the cities would raise the revenue they needed for local functions. For Roman citizens, an inheritance tax was imposed, "assessed at 5 percent on all inheritances except for gifts to children and spouses."[21] A 1 percent sales tax on all goods and 4 percent tax on slaves were enacted. Although most of the citizenry was able to "manage" with the tax burden that was introduced, Judea was rebellious. The rebellion by the Jews eventually led to the suicide of the remaining rebels at Masada (73 A.D.) where they chose death instead of succumbing to Roman taxation.

From 180 A.D. until the beginning of Diocletian's rule, the empire began a slow descent. Undermining the economy and the social fabric of Roman society was a familiar phenomenon—inflation. With a chaotic central government in Rome, the decentralization of Roman decision-making that was in place spared the outlying cities of much of the unrest that engulfed Rome. By the time Diocletian took command and introduced a policy that can be best described as uncompromising dictatorship, the question was when, not if, totalitarianism would collapse.

The moral of ancient tax policies can be summed up by Weber and Wildavsky:

> Citizens will more willingly support government if its taxes are moderate, and if taxes are administered evenhandedly by officials who maintain high standards of honesty and accountability while holding public office.[22]

Rostovtzeff is even more blunt in his assessment of the final decades of the Roman Empire.

> The reforms of Diocletian . . .by giving permanence to the policy of organized robbery on the part of the state, made all productive activity impossible. But it did not stop the formation of large fortunes, rather it contributed to their formation, while altering their character. The foundation of the new fortunes was no longer the creative energy of men, nor the discovery and exploitation of new sources of wealth, nor the improvement and development of commercial, industrial, and agricultural enterprises; it was in the main the skillful (sic) use of a privileged position in the state to cheat and exploit the state and the people alike. Public officials, both high and low, grew rich on bribery and corruption.[23]

With such a rich history to learn from, did the Roman Empire's descendants do any better in organizing and administering society than their ancestors?

The Medieval Period

A major distinguishing characteristic of medieval Europe during both the feudal and pre-feudal periods was one-man rule over a geographic territory. In essence, this structure of government meant that the controlled land—the public economy—and the private household of the local authority

were one.[24] By the time cities became more populated with
peasants after the twelfth century, a revival of the Greek
liturgy was being developed. Merchant guilds "taxed" their
"members to support construction and maintenance of public
facilities—market buildings, town clocks, roads and bridges;
the donations benefitted all town citizens as well as the
guildsmen."[25] Tax farming reappeared. Who else but the
merchant class could have undertaken this task for the feudal
monarchs? The close relationship between the merchants and
the feudal kings evolved because the monarch had the power
to grant trade concessions to the merchants in exchange for the
capital he needed for his military adventures. In short, *state
capitalism*, not *laissez-faire,* dominated early medieval socioeconomic relationships. As Rosenberg and Birdzell observe:
"The merchants and guilds wanted control of taxation and
trade to be in their own hands; they did not want an end to
taxation or the control of trade. Economic organization independent of political control was conceptually as alien to the
towns of the Middle Ages as to the manors."[26]

    The economies of medieval regions began to expand
slowly between the seventh and tenth centuries, in sharp
contrast to the subsistence economy of the fifth to seventh
centuries. (People, however, were still living in relative poverty, but compared with earlier centuries, their conditions had
improved.) The boom in agricultural productivity in the centuries before the first millennium was a double-edged sword.
As the economy grew and more people were fed, the agricultural surplus also made it possible to support a parasitic class
of feudal knights and nobles. Again, prosperity ironically
helped cultivate a parasitic class in society, which was able to
tax the surplus produced by the private sector.

    The economy of the medieval period was rapidly being
transformed. Money began to appear in ninth century England
and Gaul, while in the tenth century money was used even in
rural northern Italian districts. Towns began to see products

being imported from further distances. Fairs developed not only to sell products but also to serve as interregional financial clearinghouses. Commerce, in short, was expanding beyond anyone's forecast. Markets grew as specialization increased and distance became less of a trade barrier. Facilitating this process was, of course, the reintroduction of money—the general medium of exchange.[27]

Where there is relative prosperity, there tends to be looters and plunderers. This period was no exception. Scandinavian tribes attacked "coastal settlements of England, Ireland, Germany and France." The need for protection was obvious. As stability eventually arrived, feudal kings were able to consolidate their power, especially since they could tax and receive money in addition to in-kind payments. By receiving money they could in turn hire troops which, of course, could be used to eliminate opposition and extend their power.[28]

Nevertheless, between the eleventh and fourteenth centuries, monarchs in need of revenue faced an unexpected development which changed the equation of the sovereign and his ability to levy taxes. Now, the English monarch had to contend with baronial councils, which began to exercise their opposition to what previously had been an uncontested prerogative of the crown. After King John signed the Magna Carta, subsequent charters reinforced the documents, namely by establishing the principles that, "the king must obtain his subjects' consent before he could levy new taxes . . . [and] . . . like all other men, the king was subject to law."[29] England became a "limited monarchy."

With the barons exercising their political strength, some wealthy commoners decided "to meet as a House of Commons, to approve taxation for commoners in the same way the Great Council approved taxation for the nobility."[30] Taxation was now to be debated instead of arbitrarily imposed on all the people. And, when the king requested funds for military purposes, consent would be given only if he demonstrated that the military operations were defensive, that is, there was a real need to repel an aggressor.[31] In other words, the king was unable to tax unless he obtained the consent of Parliament. And, consent would not be forthcoming unless the king demonstrated a dire emergency existed, and the approved tax would be in effect for no more than one year. The king, therefore, did not have permanent taxing power, a blessing for society.

The separation of powers in post–Magna Carta England meant that

> . . . the king could spend but not tax, Parliament could tax but not spend. As long as the power to tax and the power to spend were separated, the rights of Englishmen would live forever, especially the right to be free from oppressive taxation. Today the principle of separation of powers means something quite different. Our current runaway taxation is the natural conse-quence of our abandonment of that ancient English practice. We live in a pre–Magna Carta world in which we—like the subjects of King John—can be pillith with taxes and tallages unto the bare bones.[32]

What if? What if the emerging European nation-states embraced the Magna Carta's principles; would European history have been different? Instead of the centralization of power in the monarchy throughout most of Europe in the Middle Ages, power—political, social, and economic—would have been diffused and the tax revolts that erupted (14th century) may have been prevented in Florence, France, and England when governments taxed the poor heavily in the aftermath of the plague. Feudalism contained the seeds of its destruction. Tyranny cannot be a long lasting thread of society's fabric. Without low taxes—in medieval Europe or in any other time period—society will be unstable.

Although living standards were improving, they were still relatively low for most of Europe between the fifteenth and eighteenth centuries. Taxes placed a huge burden on the working poor because the absolutist state taxed them very heavily. Indirect taxes—levies on goods—were particularly onerous because the poor spent virtually their entire income on consumption. In addition, the poor supplied labor services demanded by the state to build and maintain roads. Thus the most defenseless group in society was literally trampled by big government hundreds of years ago.

By the sixteenth century rulers began to flex their muscles again in Spain, France, and England, ushering in a period of absolute monarchies. With the expansion of markets, states actively intervened in order to obtain revenue and control economic activity. Although markets existed, they clearly were not free markets. In addition, in order to increase the state's power, large-scale warfare became institutionalized. This again confirms a central theme of world history; obtaining money through taxation to exercise power is the common thread of virtually all states. The masses' reaction to the absolutist state were manifested in many ways. Initially, criticism by writers, philosophers, and others provided both the philosophical opposition to absolutism and introduced an alternative to *statism*, the free market.

The Enlightenment, the period of intellectual history which questioned the "Old Order," was a lightning bolt shattering the pretense of the divine right of kings and articulating a revolutionary principle—the rights of man. In effect, all the monarch's activities were questioned, including the principles of mercantilism, which asserts that a nation is made wealthy by increasing exports and limiting imports thereby obtaining more money—a sign of wealth. In the states of Europe, governments effectively nationalized whole industries (salt, ores, and fuel), established private monopolies to extract revenue from merchants given exclusive trading rights for certain commodities, and taxed land and goods to fill the treasurers' coffers to cement mercantilism in society. Scanning the tax policies of the Middle Ages reveals that direct taxation on income was rarely implemented but taxes on consumer goods were com-

mon. Food, drink, salt, coal, candles, and soap were taxed
regularly. Material used for producing goods, such as silk,
wool fabric, leather, and whalebone also felt the taxman's
hand. Figs, tobacco, playing cards, and dice were taxed, too.
In England, country houses built by upper income families
didn't escape the taxman. Construction material was taxed and
houses were taxed according to size, thereby introducing one
of the first examples of progressive taxation.

Conclusion

More episodes of taxation in the Western world could
be examined, but the overall picture is crystal clear. Why
depress you with tales of oppression and brutality your ancestors experienced at the hands of the taxman centuries ago in
England, Spain, Prussia, Italy, Russia, etc ? History is, in the
final analysis, a struggle between the ruling elite who wants
the masses' money and the masses who want to be left alone.
The elite demand(ed) money from the citizenry as a *matter of
right*. The public, however, has to earn it first. Hence, the age-
old conflict between the robbers and the robbed. The institu-
tionalization of robbery in the hands of the state retarded
economic development, distorted production, and caused un-
told misery.[33] Throughout history, it was not that the masses
were not taxed enough to support the state apparatus, which
according to contemporary apologists of government spending is a critical link in promoting prosperity, but rather the
masses were taxed to support the opulent lifestyles of the
parasitic class in society—the rulers and their henchmen.
Economic development will occur "naturally" under a
regime of free markets. In other words, trade barriers, price
controls, depreciating money, shackled labor, all must be
eliminated for entrepreneurship, innovation, savings-investment, capital formation, employment opportunities, and consumption to flourish. The argument that government must

intervene in the marketplace to promote economic growth is
dispelled by centuries of history. Ignoring several thousand
years of human experience on this planet of state ownership of
industry or control of commerce leads one to question the
intelligence—and knowledge—of statism's supporters.

In non–European societies, taxation caused economic
havoc and social unrest, too. In the Ottoman Empire (mid-
sixteenth century), high taxes caused the people to flee,
leading to the depopulation of vast areas. Peasants were taxed
heavily to enrich the ruling elite, public officials and military
officers. In surveying seventeenth century India, one analyst
cited the subjugation of the common people because of the
"parasitic" actions of the tax collectors (policemen). In some
instances, the tax rate reached 50 percent![34]

The brief history and overview of taxation reveals
conclusively that the state did not limit its actions to protecting
the lives and property of its citizens—the foremost duty of a
moral state. Once the state steps beyond its protective role,
social unrest is virtually inevitable. The French Revolution is
a case in point. The fiscal crisis that engulfed France was
another example of a nation-state living beyond its means,
which culminated in an overthrow of the *ancien regime*.
Again, the tax burden fell mainly on small farmers and
workers, groups that were financially unable to purchase
"titles" which would have exempted them from some taxes.[35]
Merchants, bankers, traders, financiers, builders, engineers,
lawyers, doctors, educators, and farmers have been quite
capable of undertaking their respective duties and responsibilities within a rational legal framework to improve the
public's living standards. The heavy hand of the state has been
shown to oppress primarily the lowest income groups in
society. Today, the same is being done, but the tax action is
rationalized in the name of helping the poor and downtrodden.

The American Experience

The Colonial Period

With the establishment of the first English settlement at Jamestown, Virginia in 1607, the British colonial period began in the New World. Who knew that from this humble beginning the American Revolution would occur 170 years later, creating the United States of America, a nation "conceived in liberty" that epitomized the antithesis of the Old Order of feudalism, monopoly, special privileges, etc. No sooner had the settlers arrived along the east coast and began to organize themselves in small towns when the colonists in Massachusetts undertook the first tax strike (1631) to protest the assessment for the construction of frontier forts. The citizens of Watertown asserted that they were not subject to taxation "on the great old English ground that no community may be taxed without its consent."[36] The colonial government withdrew the tax and established a more democratic form of governance. A fundamental principle was thus established, at least in Massachusetts; taxes must be approved by the people or their representatives.

In Virginia, meanwhile, Sir William Berkeley began serving as governor in 1642 and continued until 1677, with only a brief interruption. Initially, Berkeley repealed the poll tax and taxes on estates were reduced. Previously, Governor Harvey had imposed "export taxes on tobacco and fees on each immigrant." In 1635, the colonists rebelled at Harvey's despotic rule, and they shipped him back to England. However, he returned in 1637 and began confiscating his enemies' property and also intended to impose a tithing tax on corn of the parishioners of one of his staunchest enemies. Finally, the Crown removed Harvey in 1639 and his successor "was instructed to convene periodic meetings of the Virginia Assembly, thereby making Virginia's representative body a permanent one."[37]

In England, Charles I was executed by Parliament (1649) and the Virginia Assembly denounced the execution and defied Parliament. Parliament retaliated in 1650 and passed the first Navigation Act, which imposed strict trade restrictions on the colony. Virginia was now forbidden to trade with foreign countries or engage in commerce with "foreign ships lacking a special license."[38] Needless to say, Virginians were quite upset and the assembly proclaimed, in effect, that they were going to defy Parliament's edicts. Parliament reacted by sending a commission to squash the colony's defiance, but instead of imposing severe punishment, the commissioners removed Governor Berkeley and allowed the House of Burgesses, the colony's elected delegate body, to become the governing power. In the House of Burgesses, therefore, the legislative executive, and judicial power would now be centered. The colony also was to be "free from all taxes, customs and impositions" and that future taxes could only be imposed with the consent of the assembly.[39]

Mercantilist policies continued unabated in England. The Navigation Act of 1673 imposed a one penny tax on intercolony tobacco trade and customs commissioners were appointed to collect the duty. Trade with New England was thus severely affected.

Virginia also began to practice mercantilism to offset the drop in tobacco prices, which resulted from both the rise in production and drop in trade because of the Navigation Acts. Virginia believed that by creating a compulsory cartel, prices could be raised. Governor Berkeley, who was returned to office in 1660, did a 180-degree turn, and reimposed the poll tax (1673), which greatly burdened the poor. He also had virtually taken control of the colony's government with support of the wealthy planter oligarchy and thus ruled Virginia with an iron fist. The people of Virginia were thus accumulating grievances against the colonial government for nearly fifteen years when a tax protest was organized in Surry County in late 1673. The leaders were hauled into court and exorbitant fines were levied for their "seditious acts," namely their refusal to pay these unjust taxes. Berkeley remitted the fines after the public overwhelmingly felt the tax rebels were unfairly treated.

As we surveyed the history of taxation, the relationship between war and taxes is eminently obvious. So, too, was it in Virginia. Briefly, Virginia had both hostile and friendly relations with the Indians early in its history. Hostilities, however, accelerated after colonists "poisoned two hundred Indian leaders and shot fifty others" at a peace parlay in 1623.[40] After the 1646 peace treaty, the Indians were forbidden to enter certain areas, while trade could be conducted at specified forts. Some forts, moreover, had the monopoly trade rights with the Indians, and not surprisingly, taxes were needed to construct the forts as well as support the troops once they were stationed there.

The peace with the Indians was shaky as settlers moved westward, so by 1656 trade with the Indians was virtually unrestricted. When Berkeley resumed the governorship, he effectively eliminated free trade with the Indians and reestablished trading monopolies. Hostilities with some of the Indian tribes resumed and plantations near the Indian areas were raided. Governor Berkeley then decided to erect more forts in a defensive maneuver. The settlers on the frontier, however, were intent on full-scale war with the Indians and viewed Berkeley as "being soft on the Indians." In addition, Berkeley had a monopoly of the fur trade with the Indians. The prominent anti-Berkeley leader was twenty-eight year old Nathaniel Bacon, Jr.[41]

The stage was now set for Bacon's Rebellion, which was a precursor to the American Revolution, not because of Bacon's devotion to liberty, but because of his revolutionary zeal. Although Bacon seized power in order to fight the Indian raids, he regrettably favored total independence from England because his rebellion against Berkeley meant he was also rebelling against the Crown. He nevertheless introduced some pro-liberty measures including prohibiting an individual from holding two offices, electing freemen annually, and generally making the government more open and democratic. Bacon, unfortunately, also enacted harsh measures such as liquor sales restrictions, corn export prohibitions, and more Indian regulations.

In the final analysis, events apparently overtook Bacon and his followers, who, in airing some grievances against the governor, soon realized it was either independence or continued imperial rule. There was to be no middle way.

The revolution was short-lived. Bacon died on 26 October 1676, after only a few months as head of Virginia. After Bacon's colleagues were captured, Berkeley hanged the leaders, but not before Anthony Arnold, in an eloquent address, attacked the rights of kings. When the king's commissioners came to Virginia to sort out the events, they surprisingly granted the rebels a pardon and relayed the king's order to Berkeley that he return to England. Defiant, Berkeley seized more property and hanged more rebels. The commissioners soon realized Berkeley had to be removed in order for peace to occur. Meanwhile, the people saw the unfolding events as an opportunity to redress their grievances, namely, the high taxes for expenditures they had no control over. In May 1677, Berkeley finally left for England, where he died soon after arriving. But, in Virginia his death was still unknown and Berkeley's clique continued to harass the rebels in court and imposed additional poll taxes which, of course, placed a heavy burden on the poorest citizens. When news of Berkeley's death reached the colony, the king's general pardon was published and the rebels in hiding returned to Virginia life. However, Berkeley's system remained in place. Thus, although the rebellion failed, a mighty rebellion one hundred years later was to prove successful.

Throughout the colonies, taxes were imposed and *quitrents* (property taxes paid in lieu of feudal services) on all landowners were levied by the proprietor. The latter, a remnant of feudalism, were raised periodically to as much as quadruple the previous rate, and then reduced or not enforced because of the fierce opposition. In addition, some colonies enacted poll taxes, which occasionally were used to support a particular ministry, adding to some colonies' grievances against government. That the colonists were sensitive to taxes is one of the great understatements about the colonial period. A complete examination of the colonists' experiences with taxation would indeed be lengthy and instructive, but one specific episode highlights how a society can function without a governmental apparatus, in short, without taxation.

In 1681, William Penn was granted a charter for the land called Pennsylvania, thereby canceling the king's debt to Penn's father. The charter called for the proprietor (Penn) to rule with the "advice and consent of an assembly of freemen."[42] Penn began selling land after his arrival in the fall of 1682 and tried to impose quitrents which he found difficult to collect.

As a haven for Quakers seeking religious liberty, Pennsylvania also became a colony noted for its peaceful relations with the Indians. It is all the more remarkable considering the hostile Indian-settler relationships that were unfolding in other colonies.

Taxes were low in Pennsylvania; liquor and cider were taxed as well as general goods, while an export duty on hides and furs also raised some revenue. Penn was told by some of Pennsylvania's leaders that development would be achieved faster if taxes were held down. Shades of supply-side economics! Penn went even further, suspending taxes for a year, then trying to raise taxes, which the assembly refused to do. When Penn returned to England, the freedom he allowed in the colony was soon to take on significant features. In Penn's absence, the people of Pennsylvania did not vote for taxes and stopped paying quitrents. So during 1684-88, government virtually ceased to exist in Pennsylvania; it became a taxless society. Trade was thriving because the people were also violating the oppressive Navigation Acts.

Pennsylvania's experiment in self-government was in its infancy and a worried William Penn was not able to obtain revenue for himself as his fortune began dwindling. In April 1692, the council passed a bill to reestablish taxes, which was a minimal amount, even for the citizens of Pennsylvania. The assembly, however, did not pass the tax bill. Penn appealed to the Quakers for a ten thousand pound loan. They refused.

A split developed within the Quakers' ranks, and the majority faction began to persecute their rivals. Meanwhile, the new king, William III, named new governors of both New York and Pennsylvania in late 1692. One of the new governors' first tasks was to reimpose taxes to obtain funds to fight against New France (War and taxes!). The Pennsylvania Assembly reluctantly passed a tax bill, and a taxless society ceased to exist. Statism reared its ugly head once again with a vengeance in a society that was at peace, prospering, and had established liberty.

In the eighteenth century up until 1763, the colonies basically enjoyed a stable period, which ironically coalesced the disparate settlements into coherent loose union which made the American Revolution possible. As the colonies were relatively unburdened by England because of a policy of "salutary neglect" they were able "to flourish in virtual *de facto* independence from the mother country."[43]

But, with the end of the French and Indian War in America (1763), Britain was now able to turn its attention to the colonies, which prospered under the relative *laissez-faire* policy of the English government under the control of the Whigs. Now, with the Tories in power, mercantilist policies were enacted. After all, colonies are to be exploited, and the English government was about to embark on a policy that literally would change the course of world history.

A summary of the events leading to the American Revolution has been succinctly described by economist Murray Rothbard in Volume II of his multivolume history of the American Colonies.

> The fundamental attitude of England toward its colonies was one of imperial domination, regulation, and exploitation for the benefit of the merchants and manufacturers of the imperial center. The basic mercantilist structure was built up by the Navigation Acts during the seventeenth century, even before Britain was in a position to attempt to enforce these regulations. The aim was to benefit English trade, and to supply the home country with raw material, but always for the enhancement of the English merchant or manufacturer. The means for a growing network of restrictions and prohibitions to be enforced by the arm of the state.[44]

Couple the objective conditions of the colonists' experience with the philosophical critiques that were being penned in both England and the colonies, and all the ingredients of a successful revolution were beginning to fall into place.

The point that needs to be emphasized again and again is that taxes are not only direct payments individuals make to the state, but also deprivations that people suffer because of the state's restrictions in the marketplace. In other words, taxes can either be direct, income, poll, etc., and also indirect, in the form of trading prohibitions, and monopoly grants to favored individuals or groups. Thus, the only policy that establishes a "level playing field" in the marketplace, is for the government not to meddle in economic relationships people want to engage in voluntarily. Any attempt by the government to influence economic activity automatically "taxes" some—or many—people for the benefit of others.

The history of taxation in the American colonies underscores how statism led to a revolt by the masses and the creation of a nation founded on the principles of limited government, individual liberty, and minimal taxation. As we review the tax policies of the nineteenth and early twentieth centuries, we shall see how eventually the American revolutionaries' descendants betrayed their ancestors.

United States Taxation: 1789-1913

Direct taxation was an anathema to the citizens of the United States. Sure, minimal taxes or other levies were used to fund the proper functions of government, but the key for Americans was to reach a consensus on the proper role of government. However, since the new nation was saddled with a war debt because the Continental Congress (1775–1781) and the Articles of Confederation were precluded from taxing the people (a power that was felt should be left to the states), a constitutional convention was called to address this and other issues. With the power to tax codified in the new Constitution, the door to national taxation became a possibility, an irony that would have widespread ramifications for the next one hundred years.

The new Constitution enumerated both specific and general powers of the federal government and also delegated to the states or the people responsibilities not specifically outlined in the document. With a constitutional republic in place, the United States embarked on a historic journey, keeping governmental power in check in a world where nation-states exercised extensive control over their citizens. The American experiment in limited government was about to begin.

An income tax was unthinkable in the young republic, especially after the colonies had revolted against indirect taxes, so the idea of having direct taxes on income was not even contemplated. The income tax, however, became a reality in 1862 under President Lincoln, who instituted the first income tax during the Civil War (When else?). Ironically, the tax was introduced to raise revenue to fight a war, not against a foreign threat, but against another section of the country—the South!

The Civil War was one of the opening shots in the federal government's assault on the American people. For, as we have seen, war requires money and the federal government in this instance thought it could raise it quickly by direct taxation. The first income tax was a "flat three percent of net income over $600 a year." In other words, a flat tax. Revenues were insufficient and in two years a graduated income tax was introduced. In 1864, the maximum rate was pegged at 10 percent and the tax code was made much more complex with the addition of special provisions, exceptions, etc. Inasmuch as a direct tax was prohibited by the Constitution unless it was apportioned among the states, the Lincoln administration called its income tax an excise tax. Opposition to the income tax came from both Republicans and Democrats. One Northern Democrat not only opposed the war, a heroic position at the time, but called Lincoln a dictator and denounced his income tax policy in these words.

> Through a tax law, the like of which has never been imposed upon any but a conquered people, they (the Republicans) have possession . . . of the entire property of the people of the country.[45]

To call the country's first federal income tax unpopular is a gross understatement. Although the Supreme Court upheld the constitutionality of the income tax in 1868, it was finally repealed in 1872. The vote in the Congress was instructive. New England states and California voted overwhelmingly for repeal, while fourteen southern and western states and New Hampshire voted nearly unanimously to maintain the tax. The New England states and California had paid 70 percent of the tax; in contrast, the South and West (and New Hampshire) paid only 11 percent. Self-interest of the citizens in the respective sections of the country undoubtedly played a role in the vote for repealing the income tax.

The federal government's chains on the American people were broken, for now. The post–Civil War era of reconstruction and healing was underway, as well as the economic boom that occurred throughout the 1866–1913 period, although the boom was interrupted occasionally by downturns caused by unsound monetary policies. Nevertheless, regional rivalries continued in the political arena because tariffs and excise taxes, the primary revenue sources of the federal government, were considered oppressive by some sections of the country.

Probably more important than the political jockeying between the Northeast and South and West was the serious discussion by some writers, philosophers, economists, and others who favored an income tax in the post–Civil War period. In order to enact legislation, especially a radical bill, there usually is some grand philosophical justification cited by the proponents in order to rally support. Although the income tax, particularly a progressive tax, had very little public support, some economists embraced the tax not because of a "soak the rich philosophy" but as a sound way to raise governmental revenue that would rise and fall with private incomes. Amasa Walker, for example, a staunch advocate of *laissez-faire*, nonetheless wanted an income tax and the repeal of virtually all indirect taxes because they were very unequal, unjust, and expensive.[46] Christian Socialists, meanwhile, generally favored taxing the wealthy to reduce disparities in income. They supported taxes on real estate on a graduated scale, inheritance taxes, etc.

Although the income tax was supported by individuals across the ideological spectrum, the public was not swayed. Professional economists, meanwhile, had formed the American Economic Association under the leadership of Richard Ely who "stressed the need to abandon extreme laissez-faire and to humanize economics." Not surprisingly, Ely had studied in Germany before returning to the United States in 1880, was a Christian Socialist, and favored more regulation of business to help workers in the factories. Although many of the leading economists would have liked to have had an income tax enacted, they felt the time was not ripe for such a radical proposal.

The income tax was a heretical idea to Americans in general, especially when U.S. citizens may have contemplated that one of the ten planks in Karl Marx's *Communist Manifesto* (1848) proposes "a heavy progressive or graduated income tax." How many Americans know this today? The income tax was considered by Marx as a means to socialize and eventually communize society. But, as we saw, even advocates of *laissez-faire* supported an income tax, albeit a minimal one (1/2 to 3 percent) while exempting most working people from paying any tax. So support of an income tax does not make one *ipso facto* a Marxist.

The stage was now set for an income tax to be passed by Congress as a revenue-raising measure in order to lower tariffs that raised prices of imported goods and hence were an undue burden on the poor and low-income families. In addition, the South and West welcomed an income tax to replace the high tariffs which were undermining their respective economies. The impetus for an income tax in 1894 probably was the Panic of 1893 that led to the depression of the nineties. (It ended in 1897.) Meanwhile, in the 1892 presidential campaign, both the People's Party and the Socialist Labor Party called for a graduated income tax. The political support for an income tax also came from the Greenback Party and in 1884 the Anti-Monopoly Party also called for a graduated income tax. The ghost of Karl Marx was hovering over America! Grover Cleveland was elected in 1892 after losing the 1888 election. He had already served one term in the White House (1885-1889). Cleveland, a pro-gold Democrat, wanted lower tariffs, an issue that swept him to victory in 1892 because of the McKinley Tariff that passed in 1890. The public sentiment was clear, high tariffs were harming us.[47]

Income tax fever was rising. The Populist Party was gaining supporters in the West and South. The momentum in Congress to repeal the McKinley Tariff Act was unstoppable. With enough votes to pass the Wilson-Gorman Tariff bill, the Populists in Congress added an amendment that provided for an income tax. Opposition to the income tax was led by Senator David Hill of New York, who chronicled why the income tax should not be enacted. He asserted that the income tax would put the burden of running the government on a very small number of people; it would give the government inquisitorial powers, and it would take the U.S. down the road to *socialism*, just like European nations. Cleveland, nevertheless, let the bill become law without his signature because he opposed the personal income tax amendment.

The proponents of an income tax won the initial battle temporarily. The amendment called for a 2 percent tax on all incomes above four thousand dollars, including dividends, interest, rents, sales of real estate and property, and gifts. Interest on federal bonds that had been issued with a prior exemption were tax exempt. Interestingly, the salaries of state and local officials, federal judges, and the president were also exempt.[48]

In 1895, a challenge to the income tax provision reached the Supreme Court in *Pollock v. Farmer's Loan and Trust Company*. One of the major issues examined by the Court was the precedent of the Civil War income tax, namely, that a direct tax did not have to be levied without apportionment according to population. In its first decision, the Court ruled that taxes on real estate income were a direct tax that was not apportioned and hence unconstitutional, and taxes on state

and municipal bonds were also unconstitutional. The Court
split 4–4 on the constitutionality of the income tax *per se* and
a rehearing was requested with the full nine member court.
The Court, in a 5–4 decision, ruled the income tax unconstitutional. The Court heard arguments that the income tax was an
assault on property rights, and in a concurring opinion, Justice
Stephen Field, the senior member of the Court cited the
income tax as "an assault upon capital . . . [and just] the
beginning. It will be but the stepping stone to others, larger and
more sweeping, till our political contests will become a war of
the poor against the rich, a war constantly growing in intensity
and bitterness."[49] In his dissent, Justice John Harlan proved to
be omniscient. He argued that it would now take a constitutional amendment to tax property and incomes in order to
support the national government.

The opponents of a federal income tax won a great
victory for nineteen years. After the Supreme Court's decision, the income tax issue remained dormant even though the
1896 Democratic platform included an income tax plank, and
the usual pro-tax suspects—the Populist and Socialist Labor
parties—also called for an income tax. The 1896 Democratic
ticket was headed by the "prairie" Populist, William Jennings
Bryan. In short, the Democratic party no longer was to represent the limited government, low-tax party in the United
States. Instead, the Democrats became proponents of massive
government intervention, a betrayal of their Jeffersonian-
Jacksonian legacy. In his first annual message to Congress,
Thomas Jefferson urged repeal of all internal taxation, and
Andrew Jackson in his Farewell Address stated that any
money taken from the people by the Congress beyond the
amount needed to undertake the specific powers granted by the
Constitution "is an abuse of the power of taxation and unjust
and oppressive."[50] How soon political parties forget their
philosophical foundation!

Populism was gaining strength but still could not garner enough support to elect William Jennings Bryan president in 1896, 1900, or 1908. Meanwhile, so-called insurgents in both major political parties were calling for tariff and tax reform. President Theodore Roosevelt indicated support for an income tax plus an inheritance tax in 1906. The tariff came under attack again because rising prices since the late 1890s had made the cost of foreign goods a hot political issue. William Howard Taft, Roosevelt's successor in the 1908 campaign, defeated Bryan who lost for the third time. Taft indicated his support for an income tax, and soon threw his weight (No pun intended; he weighed over 300 pounds!) behind a new tariff bill in March 1909, which was amended to include an income tax. In June, President Taft issued a statement endorsing a constitutional amendment that could give the country a permanent income tax. (Legislation would still be needed, however, to set the rates, establish a tax collection mechanism, etc., even if the Constitution was amended.) In addition, a 2 percent tax on corporate net income was also proposed in the tariff bill. With the bill's passage in July 1909, a corporate income tax became permanent, but the income tax now had to be ratified by three-fourths of the state legislatures for the Sixteenth Amendment to become the law of the land.

The Sixteenth Amendment was not ratified until February 1913. Predictably, some southern states voted to ratify as early as 1909, and many eastern states also ratified the amendment, even New York, which did so in 1911 after Democrats won control of the legislature and the governorship. Under Republican governor Charles Evans Hughes, the New York State legislature failed to ratify, even though the governor personally favored passage of the amendment, but expressed concern that the tax would be levied on state and municipal bonds. With New York state balking, other states

probably held back ratification until the state finally ratified
the amendment after the Democrats' victory in the 1910
election.

A PROFIT

Meanwhile, in Virginia, Richard E. Byrd, the Speaker
of the House of Delegates, feared that the Sixteenth Amendment would extend the federal government's power over
every American citizen.

> A hand from Washington will be stretched out and placed
> upon every man's business; the eye of the inspector will be in
> every man's counting house . . . the law will of necessity have
> inquisitorial features, it will provide penalties, it will create
> complicated machinery. Under it men will be hauled into court
> distant from their homes. Heavy fines imposed by distant and
> unfamiliar tribunals will constantly menace the tax payer. An
> army of Federal inspectors, spies, and detectives, will descend
> upon the state . . .[51]

If Speaker Byrd were alive today, what would he think
of the IRS, tax rates, etc.?

After the secretary of state certified the adoption of the
Sixteenth Amendment on 25 February 1913, newspapers
editorialized: "He has a mean spirit who objects to an income
tax"; "The prospect of many millions of new revenue should
give the tariff-makers a much freer hand in so readjusting
duties as to produce the greatest possible benefit to the consumer"; "This is the most objectionable of all forms of taxes";
"It is wrong in principle and un-American in spirit."[52]

The election to the presidency of Democrat New
Jersey Governor Woodrow Wilson in 1912 paved the way for
an income tax bill to become law in 1913. Congress was called
into special session in April and the Underwood Tariff was
proposed, which included a reduction in tariff rates along with
an income tax. The income tax portion of the bill called for a
$4,000 exemption for married couples ($3,000 for single
taxpayers), a 1 percent tax on incomes up to $20,000, and

graduated surtaxes increasing 6 percent for incomes up to $500,000. In short, the maximum rate was 7 percent—chicken feed compared with what was to follow over the next eighty years.

The nation's first peacetime, permanent income tax became law on 3 October 1913. Other major provisions included: income from local and state bonds were tax exempt, as were the salaries of all state and local employees; both the president's income and that of federal judges were untaxed; taxes on gifts and inheritances were excluded from the law, however a separate inheritance tax was under consideration.

In 1914, $28 million was collected, $41 million in 1915, and nearly $68 million in 1916. Only 2 percent of the U.S. population paid the federal income tax between 1914 and 1915. No sooner had the proponents of taxation asserted that the rates would remain "low" and only be paid by wealthy Americans, the maximum rate was hiked to "15 percent in 1916, 67 percent in 1917, and 77 percent in 1918."[53] Wartime need for revenue pushed rates to levels that may even have embarrassed the most pro-income tax advocates. But, all's fair in love and war, and World War I was no exception. During World War II, the top marginal rate reached 94 percent! Six cents for you, ninety-four cents for Uncle Sam, if you earned at least $200,000. Who said the government didn't know how to enter into partnerships that make organized crime look like candidates for sainthood? Such "takings" must have made Jefferson, Jackson, and their followers want to rise from the dead and knock some sense into the heads of federal government officials.

What should we make of the income tax becoming a part of American society and thus establishing the first leg of quasi-socialism in the nation? To conclude that the income tax was inevitable is to embrace determinism and not the conscious decision-making of federal lawmakers who were influenced by various forces throughout the period. But, probably the most underestimated factor during the discussion of the income tax and other public policies was the attitude and actions of the business community. The business community, especially in the Northeast, supported the protective tariff in order to build up their new industries and reap enormous profits, which could only be accomplished at the expense of consumers who were faced with higher-priced goods. The so-called infant industry argument (protecting new industries from competition so they could get established in the market-place) cloaked their naked use of the government to effectively stifle foreign competition in the country. This touched off virtually continuous protests by various groups, culminating in the grand coalition that agitated for a federal income tax, which was seen both as a welcome replacement for high tariffs and a necessary levy based on the "ability to pay." In short, the great wealth that had been accumulated during the industrial-ization of the country was basically untaxed and the income tax was seen as a way to tap this wealth and thus reduce the tax burden on the vast majority of the people. Clearly, the propo-nents of the income tax had a valid case, at least in one respect: the post–Civil War tax structure was regressive, having been based on customs duties and excise taxes.[54]

Not surprisingly, "the major opposition to a federal income tax came from spokesmen for the nation's industrial, commercial and financial leaders."[55] Despite the resources at their disposal and allies in the newspapers, the march toward an income tax seemed unstoppable by 1909. And, playing a subsidiary role in the eventual passage of the Sixteenth Amend-ment was another factor that must be identified—envy. Ac-cording to one analyst, "it is significant that while westerners had sought a federal income tax since the Civil War, almost no western state had enacted its own income tax. *The target was clearly eastern wealth.*" [56] In addition, feeding at the public trough also reared its head. "Western sympathy for a federal income tax was fortified considerably because it was one region in the nation that openly sought federal aid for its development. The only feasible way to develop its resources without becoming more beholden to eastern finance was to tax the federal treasury."[57] In the South, similar attitudes were expressed by some, especially since the region was relatively depressed compared with the Northeast; the income tax was seen as a way of shifting the tax burden to wealthy easterners. Nevertheless, there was a formidable opposition to the income tax in the South from iron, steel, sugar, and textile interests who benefitted from a high protective tariff. The South's economic elite, on the other hand, exercised their influence through the "Bourbons," politicians who favored "low taxes, minimal regulation of business, and a dearth of public expenditures for social needs."[58] Thus, skepticism of federal power was strong in the South—the memory of the Civil War and its chaotic aftermath still lingering in the hearts and minds of southerners. However, growing support for federal aid to assist the region's agricultural base turned the tide for ratification in many states. The South, too, jumped on what it believed was in the offing, a gravy train from Washington D.C. to assist its economy.

As a political measure, the income tax became possible because Populists wanted more "equality." Urban representatives realized that the tariff was indeed hurting their constituencies and an income tax on the wealthy would offer some relief to consumers, and thus maybe the most controversial, "businessmen who preferred predictability" in government affairs.[59] Although publicly most businessmen opposed the income tax, there was an undercurrent of support for more government involvement in the economy, especially if they would reap some of the largesse. As Robert Higgs argues:

> The novelty of the early twentieth century was the undisguised position taken by a growing number of businessmen (especially among the Eastern elite) that government

should intervene more actively in the affairs of business (particularly by corporate business) and that, the intervention should be ongoing and institutionalized. Big businessmen's ceremonial obeisance to laissez-faire increasingly fell into desuetude, replaced by a Progressive avowal that government cease to be only a referee, that it must be a player as well.[60]

That the business community paid lip service to free markets while overtly or covertly supporting more government intervention should lay to rest the proposition that businessmen are *ipso facto* anti-government, anti-regulation, anti-subsidies, or anti-encroachment. In fact, a case could be made that big business helped deliver quasi-socialism to America. As ironic as that proposition is, consider the salient observation of Frank Chodorov.

> . . .the idea that government would give up tariff revenue in exchange for income tax revenue was contrary to all experience . . . the nature of government is such that it cannot give up one power for another; not permanently, at any rate.[61]

Furthermore,

> The Fordney-McCumber Tariff Act of 1922 (with an average ad valorem rate of 33.22 percent) restored the high protective tariff of pre-income tax days. Ironically, the agricultural bloc of the Middle West and the South that had fought for the income tax, to enable a reduction in tariffs, joined with their erstwhile opponents to enact the bill.[62]

There we have it. The American people were sucked into the bosom of big government with the promise that tariffs would decline and income taxes would only be levied on the wealthy. From our perspective in the 1990s, when will the people learn that government by nature wants to grow and grow and grow at the expense of the public. Maybe the above presentation will be the American people's wake-up call.

3

The Impact of Taxation

Taxation under every form presents but a choice of evils.

--David Ricardo

There is no art which one government sooner learns of another than the draining of money from the pockets of the people.

--Adam Smith

Taxes separate people from their money and pit citizens against each other, thereby undermining social cohesion. Taxes, therefore, are divisive. Taxation is "legal plunder." According to Bastiat, "legal plunder occurs ". . . if the law takes from some persons what belongs to them and gives it to other persons to whom it does not belong . . . if the law benefits one citizen at the expense of another by doing what the citizen himself cannot do without committing a crime."[1] Legal plunder has existed throughout history as we have shown in the last chapter, and was given sanction by the United States in 1913. (The Constitution, however, in Article I, Section 8 does give Congress the power "to lay and collect taxes, duties, imports and excises." Presumably, this would be used for legitimate government functions, defense and other law-enforcing activities. The thought of an all-encompassing income tax was abhorrent to the Founders, probably even to the most ardent supporters of a strong, central government.)

When legal plunder exists, a society's moral compass is impaired because the law in effect sanctions state robbery and theft—taxation. In other words, the government can legally do what the law rightfully prevents private individuals from doing, namely, plundering their neighbors. Moreover, when the government taxes, it is then in a position to give that money to other people, tax "consumers." The recipients of the government's largesse thus share in plundered money, the same way some individuals share in the loot stolen from a bank or a home, but who did not engage in the actual plunder. To argue otherwise, that taxation is not theft, is a reflection of the moral bankruptcy of our time!

Taxation brings in revenue for government officials to dispense on a variety of programs, for "society's" benefit. NOT! Government programs may benefit some people, or even many Americans, but not everyone. But, all government programs always benefit one group of people, government officials (elected, appointed, or civil service employees). As we shall see below, taxation and government spending, in the final analysis, greatly harm the economy, and the sooner government is confined to its proper role, protecting the people from both external and internal aggression, the sooner the American people's standard of living will rise consistently. In short, we need a tax-free economy in order to have sustainable prosperity.

Since 1913, tax rates have increased spectacularly at all levels of government. One of the best measures of the public's tax burden is furnished by the Tax Foundation, which annually computes Tax Freedom Day, the time it takes an average American family to pay all its taxes. In 1993 Tax Freedom Day fell on May 3, one of the latest days ever! Welcome to quasi-socialist America! In some states, Tax Freedom Day is as much as 18 days longer than the national average. To put Tax Freedom Day in its historical perspective, in 1929 it fell on February 9, in 1949 on March 24 and in 1969,

March 30.[2] For over six decades, government has been sucking resources uninterrupted from the private sector! And they want more! What have they been inhaling?

What do the American people receive for the privilege of working up to five months a year to pay their taxes? Besides a lot of headaches, upset stomachs, anxiety attacks, and a lower standard of living, the American people have acquired a healthy distrust of government. Yet, there are enough—too many—Americans who believe that they are entitled to as many goodies as the government has to offer, and hang the cost!

We have to examine a crucial concept; how does the income tax affect the economy's output of goods and services? After all, say the proponents of tax-and-spend policies, isn't the country wealthier today than in 1913 when the permanent income tax was first introduced? And, isn't the country wealthier today even with tax rates much higher than 1913, and the overall tax burden higher than in 1913, 1929, or 1969? Doesn't this reveal that taxes do not necessarily hamper economic growth? And, thus, can't we as a nation continue to prosper despite the current level of taxation? Therefore, why should income taxes be reduced, let alone eliminated, if the economy is currently pouring out the greatest amount of goods and services in our country's history? Doesn't this prove that income taxes—and government spending—are not only not harmful, but in fact may be beneficial to the economy? And, aren't there unmet needs that can only be filled by government action?

The above represents the sum total of the argument in favor of taxation and government spending: taxes are not harmful to the economy and government must or should deliver certain services the people want. These assertions are just that, unsubstantiated statements made by power-hungry politicos and their apologists who want to rule America; in short, the rationale of America's ruling elite, just like the

Pharaohs, emperors, and kings of years gone by is more sophisticated today. They are self-described compassionate, humane souls who want to elevate the poor and low income families up the income ladder with, if necessary, other people's money. In other words, plunder is okay as long as it is done for a virtuous cause. Mind you, they, the politicians, are not going to be philanthropists with their money, but with the forced extractions from the public. Thus, politicians = phony philanthropists. Our task below is to once and for all demonstrate that our want-to-be emperors indeed have no clothes, that they are as naked philosophically as the divine rights of kings philosophy invoked throughout history by monarchs and emperors. So, let the demolition begin.

Taxes reduce (1) the individual taxpayer's standard of living, (2) the output of goods and services in the economy, and (3) the people's freedom.

The Income Tax

Every individual who pays the income tax bears the burden; in other words the tax cannot be "shifted" to his employer or anyone else. However, to the extent some workers drop out of the labor market because of the relatively low after-tax income they receive, the supply of workers will decrease. This in turn will tend to raise wages, thus "shifting" some of the income tax hikes to employees in the form of higher wages. Employees, however, still have lower incomes because of the tax. (Federal employees do not, in fact, "pay" the federal and income tax on their earnings. For example, a federal civil servant who earns $40,000 annually and "pays" $8,000 in federal taxes really earns only $32,000. As far as state and local employees are concerned, the situation is a bit more complex because state, county, and municipal governments receive a portion of their budgets from the federal government. So a state, county, or municipal employee whose income is $40,000 annually and pays $8,000 in federal taxes and, let's say, $2,000 in additional state and municipal income taxes, in effect, has a net income of $30,000. How much this public employee actually pays in federal income tax is debatable because of all the public monies flowing back and forth between the various levels of government. But, we are initially focusing our analysis on private sector employees so we do not need the focus on public employees for the time being.) Employees cannot expect to get a raise because their income taxes have increased, nor can they expect merchants to lower their prices because their net income has been reduced. However, merchants may reduce their prices because they may see their sales dropping as taxpayers' incomes decline. Nevertheless, the income tax unequivocally reduces an individual's standard of living because his net income has been reduced. Moreover, the taxpayer's future standard of living will also be reduced because of the income tax.

Our hypothetical taxpayer, for example, earns $3,000 a month, and in a tax-free society would have to pay for all the goods and services his family needs and wants, as well as providing for his retirement. (Omit for the moment about how to pay for national defense, which will be discussed in Chapter 7.) Let's assume the taxpayer consumes 90 percent of his income for food, clothing, mortgage (or rent), utilities, transportation, all insurance premiums, charitable contributions, leisure, etc.—in other words, $2,700. The remaining 10 percent, $300, is used for savings in order to provide for a retirement fund. In addition, the taxpayer may have a company sponsored retirement plan and/or health plan. There is no government Social Security program. Now, the federal government imposes a 10 percent income tax, leaving our employee with $2,700 a month net income, exactly what he was spending on consumption. But, if the taxpayer wants to save 10 percent of his income, he now would allocate his $2,700 after-tax income as follows: $2,430 for consumption, $270 for savings. Both the family's present consumption has declined and the breadwinner's future consumption probably will decline because there is 10 percent less available for savings today. However, the taxpayer may decide not to lower his after-tax consumption ($2,700) and thus forego any savings in order to maintain his current level of consumption. The income tax, therefore, will cause him to either be impoverished or have a meager standard of living during his retirement, depending entirely on friends, families, or charities. Clearly, the taxpayer will have both his current consumption and savings reduced because of the income tax.

But what about the $300 a month in taxes the government expropriates. Doesn't the taxpayer obtain benefits and services for his tax dollars? The answer is a resounding NO! First, money taken from an individual causes, as economists would say, an immediate loss of utility, for the taxpayer has less income to satisfy his wants and needs. Thus, the taxpayer is immediately worse off as soon as the tax is implemented, regardless of any "benefits" the family may receive from the government. As we shall see shortly, taxing and spending is an incredibly inefficient method to deliver services to the American people. Second, and now we shall invoke Oscar Wilde's great statement about a cynic, which we will apply to describe public officials, economists, and business executives who call for government spending and hence taxes to stimulate the economy. Wilde described a cynic as someone "who knows the price of everything and the value of nothing." This is one of the most accurate statements of the political process. When politicians propose government programs they know exactly how many tax dollars it will take to fund it, but do they know what these programs are worth to the American people? Of course not! The only method to determine the value of goods and services is to have a free market. Period. Any other method, such as the so-called democratic process, is legal plunder. When the government taxes the people to obtain funds which will be used for specific spending programs, the beneficiaries of the government's largesse are accessories before and after the fact. If they have lobbied for these programs, they are, in effect, asking the government to steal for them. The beneficiaries wouldn't—and couldn't—take money directly from the public without being branded a criminal. But, if the government does the taking, the "public" interest supposedly has been served.

The income tax has additional negative impacts. Some people may decide to work harder after the tax has been implemented so they can maintain their previous net income; for our hypothetical taxpayer that would be $300 per month. This would cause him to work either more hours in his present job or obtain another job to reach a total disposable income he previously had, $3,000 per month. There is a cost for our employee to meet this goal—loss of leisure time, less time with the family, etc. The income tax thus penalizes the worker, who in order to maintain his standard of living, has to give up time he would otherwise spend engaged in activities he desires, but now the government forces a major change in his lifestyle. In addition, taxpayers may now undertake more do-it-yourself projects because a lower disposable income makes it more expensive to hire contractors and mechanics. The economy's structure is shifted to accommodate the taxpayer at the expense of repair specialists who see their incomes decline.

The income tax lowers the return on investment. Taxes on savings accounts, certificates of deposit, stock dividends, bonds, etc., reduce the people's cash flow which would either have been reinvested and/or spent on consumption. Moreover, retirees who own these assets have a lower standard of living because of the income tax, and the working population will have a lower standard of living when they retire because the return on these assets will be taxed during their lives. Capital gains taxes have the same impact because the funds that are taxed cannot be used by the taxpayer for reinvestment and/or consumption. Moreover, the capital gains tax contains a double whammy. First, it reduces an individual's wealth and secondly it often taxes "illusory" gains. For example, if an investor bought an asset in 1972 for $100,000 and sold it in 1994 for $400,000, at first glance it appears a $300,000 capital gain has been made. Wrong! Prices quadrupled during this period, so there is exactly no gain because of the dollar's purchasing power decline between 1972 and 1994. A tax paid on this gain therefore would be taxing the capital value of the asset instead of a real gain. At minimum, capital gains taxes should be adjusted for inflation in our current tax system. Better yet, dump the tax altogether and we'll have an investment boom!

Politicians and analysts who are not in favor of lowering the capital gains tax display both their ideological colors and ignorance of economics. The former is, if not red, at least a shade of crimson and no amount of protests can alter this observation. Capital gains taxes bring in little revenue, so it is not an important revenue source for the federal government. What then is the objection to lowering the tax? Clearly, politics and ideology. Ignorance on this matter is so pervasive we won't ascribe this factor to the capital gains' existence. The capital gains tax exists because it satisfies a cardinal rule of politics: exact a pound of flesh from the "rich" otherwise the masses may be upset. This is pandering to the worst in a human being—envy. Let the editorial writers decry a lower (or zero) capital gains tax; who cares what they think? Sound economic analysis, not ideological bias or political pandering, should guide policymakers. In short, capital gains taxes must be eliminated.

The corporate income tax also falls in the category of ideological bias, political pandering, and ignorance. First, corporations do not pay taxes, only people do. That's right, a corporate income tax is a tax on shareholders, widows, orphans, retirees, lower-, middle-, and upper-income Americans, the very same people (except for the rich!) politicians state they want to "help." As my father would say about some nonsensical idea or statement, "My foot." The income tax reduces corporate cash flow available for reinvestment, thereby adversely affecting capital formation. In addition, the corporate income tax, which everyone knows, is a double taxation of business income, once at the corporate level and secondly when dividends are received by shareholders. With all the talk about "fairness," where is the outcry against the injustice?

Families can easily relate to this concept. If your child's allowance was taxed by the government after you already paid taxes on your income, would this be fair? No! So, why are shareholders being taxed on their income both as shareholders and dividend receivers? Why is corporate income taxed at all? The former is unjust and reduces shareholders' consumption and/or reinvestment, while the latter clearly undermines corporations from expanding, reinvesting, and creating more jobs. The corporate income tax must be abolished for the economy to have sustainable prosperity.

The progressive income tax, unlike the flat income tax we used as an example above, is another public policy that has its roots in Marxism. Remember, one of the ten planks in *The Communist Manifesto* called for a heavy, progressive income tax. Fortunately, our tax system is not as progressive as it seems because of exemptions, deductions, etc. If our tax system was as progressive as the scheduled rates had suggested—with marginal rates reaching 70 percent and 90 percent—the economy would indeed have suffered. How much? Who knows for sure? But, if many wealthy taxpayers had to pay those rates (and some did), less reinvestment, less work, would certainly have occurred and funds would have flowed to lower tax rate countries. With the maximum marginal rates now nearly 40 percent after the passage of the Clinton tax package of 1993, the federal government has hiked rates to "soak" the rich. This is the rallying cry of scoundrels, incompetents, and panderers.

While the progressive income tax suffers from many defects, similar to the flat or proportional tax's effect on consumption and savings as discussed above, it penalizes people for being "too" successful. What kind of message is that? It is consistent, however, with our culture's plunge into "egalitarianism." A progressive income tax, in effect, says to the people, it's okay to be successful, but if you make more than we feel comfortable with, you will have to pay a greater proportion of your income to the government. This is not only bad public policy, it is morally reprehensible. Anyone advocating a steep progressive income tax should be fitted for a strait jacket.

Punishing people for being successful in the marketplace with a progressive income tax not only tends to reduce productive activity but also breeds envy among the masses. The poor begin to believe that their plight is the result of some people having "too much income," and therefore the government should "equalize" (plunder) incomes of productive people for the benefit of lower-income groups. Redistribution of income in our society thus becomes a moral imperative and an economic necessity. Class warfare commences. The only victor is the ruling elite, both inside and outside government. To eliminate the ruling elite's stronghold on the economy, the progressive income tax must be abolished.

Other taxes that have been implemented in the past or have been considered as alternatives or supplementary to the income tax, include an accumulated capital tax, gift and inheritance taxes, and wealth taxes. All lower the people's standard of living and are, in the final analysis, indirect income taxes. All these levies are income taxes with different and fairly complex rate schedules. Taxes must be paid from current earnings (income) or accumulated earnings (wealth). Taxes cannot be paid from any other source. Thus taxation in general and "income" taxes in particular must lower both the public's present and future standard of living because of its negative effects on consumption and savings-investment.

The best succinct description of how taxation and government spending lowers the standard of living was penned by Harold J. Manley from Massachusetts in a letter to *Barron's*, the weekly financial newspaper.

> Every time a worker is moved from the private to the public payroll, you get a triple negative in our standard of living: He stops producing useful goods and services, taxes must go up to pay for the goods and services he still consumes, and he is put to work at regulating or taxing the productive economy. [3]

Truer words have not been written. Only the private sector can offer goods and services the people can value appropriately and determine their worth. Without a market for its services, our public sector suffers from the same grave defect socialist economies have tried to overcome unsuccessfully: how to allocate scarce resources efficiently without a free price system and the private ownership of the means of production. A prosperous economy can only be organized with a pervasive private sector, not with our multiple-decades-old "mixed" economy. In short, our country's ills are not the consequences of *laissez-faire*, as some left-wing critics assert, but of the inherent failings of a mixed economy. Taxation is the heart of the mixed economy because it allows government to spend a substantial portion of the productive sector's income with inevitable results—lower economic growth, economic distortions, and social instability.

The output of goods and services grows more slowly under our "mixed" tax-and-spend economy than a free economy. According to James Payne, writing in the winter 1992 issue of *Policy Review*, the U.S. tax system's burden on the economy in 1990 was—are your ready?—a staggering $618 billion. That's not a misprint, $618 BILLION! Payne estimates the amount expended by the government to administer the tax system, litigate the disputes with taxpayers, and enforce the tax laws is $5.8 billion. But, there's more. The cost to both business and individuals to comply with the tax laws is a phenomenal $232.2 billion. If that wasn't enough, the economic disincentive costs are estimated to be a mind boggling $315.6 billion. As Payne states, "This ($375.6 billion) is the value of production that is lost owing to the disincentive effect of the system."[4]

In other words, people arranged their affairs in such a way, because of federal taxes, that the output of goods and services would have been over $300 billion higher in 1990! Finally, Payne estimates (he admits with great difficulty) that tax avoidance (which is legal) and tax evasion (which is illegal) resulted in a $65 billion social cost. The public undertook many activities they otherwise wouldn't—bartering instead of using money, and thus operating their businesses less efficiently, and expanding their businesses slowly or not at all because of the desire to keep the taxman at bay. These are real costs to the economy. And yet the proponents of taxation assert that the federal tax system is relatively efficient because the government "only" spends $6 billion to collect and enforce the tax code, a cost which is pure deadweight inasmuch as tax collecting does not provide useful services to the public. Proponents of taxation make Mr. Magoo seem like an eagle-eyed fighter pilot. In fact, Mr. Magoo sees the world better than the tax proponents who claim to have a "vision" for society, but ignore the huge economic costs of taxation. Can anyone seriously argue that the costs of the tax system are inconsequential or nonexistent in light of Payne's and other analysts' evidence?

The Fairness-Freedom Issue

To speak of taxation and fairness in the same breath is to utter one of the great oxymorons of all time. Taxation is a "taking," an involuntary exchange between the citizens and the government. In short, legalized robbery. How the people are supposed to maintain their respect for the laws of a civilized society when they are systematically robbed in the name of social justice is the great illusion of Western Civilization. The public's moral strength is slowly sapped under the yoke of a tyrannical revenue system.

Slaves, serfs, and the general public throughout history have revolted because of the constant oppression of their rulers, but the oppressed, unfortunately, engaged in plunder on occasion in breaking the chains of their enslavement. People do know the difference between right and wrong, otherwise human beings could not have survived ancient or medieval times, let alone the caveman period. Law is the embodiment of right and wrong and the law, according to Bastiat, must be respected. "When law and morality contradict each other, the citizen has the cruel alternative of either losing his moral sense or losing his respect for the law."[5] By taxing people's income and establishing a complex code with myriad exclusions, deductions, exemptions, etc., some people have claimed sham deductions as a method of reducing their tax liability or have underreported their income. In other matters, they are law-abiding citizens, but as a matter of self-defense, they engage in what becomes a criminal activity. The tax code, therefore, makes criminals of ordinary citizens because taxes are perceived to be a great burden. The public's perception is what counts, not what politicians, economists, and commentators assert, namely that American people are undertaxed because taxes are higher in other countries. Today's proponents of taxation probably would have argued in the 1850s that some slaves did not have it so bad because they were whipped less frequently than other slaves!

There is no need here to criticize the Internal Revenue Service. Reams of paper have been written about the IRS's abuses, which supposedly will be a thing of the past with the Taxpayers' Bill of Rights, another oxymoron. Taxation—the income tax—and the Bill of Rights are in a fundamental conflict. The 1040 form American citizens file each year is a gross violation of—are you ready?—the public's privacy rights; financial privacy. If anti-abortion laws are a violation of a woman's right to privacy, then the tax laws certainly violate the rights of all the American people, the right to be secure in their homes and to keep their papers free from government intrusion.

The tax laws violate a basic doctrine, namely that the *people are sovereign* and the government is supposed to *protect* the people from aggressors. The federal government is not supposed to become the prime violator of the American people's fundamental rights of life, liberty, and the pursuit of happiness. To argue in favor of the nation's tax laws is basically to assert the government has a legal claim on the people's income and that the rate of taxation could reach 100 percent if the government deemed it appropriate. There is, in short, no legal restraint on the level of taxation the federal government can impose on the American people. This is an open invitation to a future tyrant who, of course, would not openly advocate enormously higher taxes. But, the government apparatus is in place for taxes to skyrocket if a "national emergency" is cited in the years ahead.

With liberty having been diminished markedly in America since 1913, who will help turn back the clock to pre–1913 America, an income-tax-free society that prospered for many decades? Although America has prospered since 1913, even with the marginal tax rates reaching 90 percent, the economy has prospered despite the tax burden because of the vitality of the private sector (the productive sector), not because of government tax-and-spend policies. In fact, as the 1990s unfold, the final chapter is being written about America's flirtation with "democratic socialism."

The crisis we face is the burden of both government spending, at an all-time high, and the tax burden, the greatest in history. By any measure, the U.S. economy has become the most socialistic in its 200 year history. The collapse of both socialism and the welfare state economies is a lesson for all—command economies do not deliver the goods and they create widespread misery. Semi-socialism does not work any better: living standards have been stagnant and an economic crisis is unfolding before our eyes.

Other Forms of Plunder

As we saw in the last chapter, the tax collector is like the rabbit in the battery commercial, he keeps going and going and going. Consequently, escaping, avoiding, and evading taxes has been a favorite pastime of people in all parts of the world since time immemorial. (The Italians, for example, have elevated tax avoidance and tax evasion to an art form.) Taxes have been levied on incomes, products, wealth, individual citizens (poll tax), slaves, animals, land, houses, inheritances, etc. Virtually nothing has escaped the taxman's reach. World history can therefore be summed up: The taxman cometh to taketh away and the people have paid until they have revolted. Rulers apparently have thought their subjects would meekly submit to their oppression forever. Wrong. Revolts, rebellions, resistance, and riots have been the inevitable consequences of taxation. If the people perceive their situation to be hopelessly oppressive, they will revolt. In democracies, the ruling elite has a safety valve—elections. Some of the rascals are thrown out periodically and taxes are rolled back marginally to satisfy the masses temporarily. But eventually even this relief wears thin.

Currently, public officials in the United States debate who should be taxed and at what rate, not whether we should fund government services with taxes. Instead, legislators debate how much government spending should increase rather than which services or programs should be privatized or eliminated. The U.S. Congress, although a representative body of all the people, has been captured by special interests in order to plunder the citizenry to satisfy the narrow objectives of the hundreds of factions in the country. This social-political structure is untenable, and is a prescription for economic disaster unless a major overhaul of the federal government occurs.

State and local governments, meanwhile, levy property and sales taxes and many large- and medium-sized cities also impose income taxes on their citizens. These taxes are used to pay for services provided by these units of government. As we shall see, these taxes reduce the people's standard of living in general while shifting money from some individuals to other citizens. This is nothing more than a massive transfer of wealth.

Property Taxes

Property taxes can be imposed on real estate structures and land and/or real personal property, equipment, animals, etc. Some of the American colonies taxed such items as cattle and slaves, justifying the levies on the principle that the greater the wealth an individual owns, the greater the ability to pay taxes. Frequently, that was not the case, especially when poor farmers had to pay in money and were unable to meet their tax obligations because they earned very little cash in the marketplace. They were essentially subsistence farmers with very little, if any, "surplus" cash. Property taxes, therefore, posed a serious problem for the colonial governments. Since there were very few "services" government had to offer, there was not a great need for revenue. Thus, there was a check on taxation in general, except for the occasional attempt to soak the colonists. Moreover, government activities were fairly limited; the idea of a pervasive welfare state was not generally accepted. The important lesson of the colonial experience is instructive. Developing countries need very low taxes in order to grow so profits can be reinvested in capital goods. By keeping taxes extremely low, the colonies and then the United States grew spectacularly throughout the nineteenth century and early twentieth century.

The property tax has become the primary source of revenue for local governments to fund schools, libraries, roads, sewers, etc. States occasionally have continued to tax non-real estate property, but have confined themselves to taxing mostly personal or corporate property, automobiles, equipment, inventory, etc. State property taxes are indeed rare today. Taxing intangible personal property, stocks, bonds, etc., was abandoned years ago because it was an administrative nightmare.

Property is a relatively easy target for the taxman because it cannot be moved. Try picking up a building or house and moving to a low-tax location. Occasionally, a small building or house has been moved to another location in a city or town in order to make room for a redevelopment project or highway. Taxing real estate at the local level can bring howls from the people if taxes are raised markedly. But, what can taxpayers do? They cannot hide the property. They cannot move their structures to another jurisdiction; they can, however, protest. Witness the property tax limitation movements in California and Massachusetts of the late 1970s. Or, as a final act of desperation, property owners could "walk" away from the property (which has occurred in many cities) leading to urban decay. But, property owners could sell the property for whatever the market will bear. In any event, property taxes tend to reduce the capital value of real estate assets, all other things being equal, of course.

Taxes on real estate—land structures—are levied on the assessed value of both residential and commercial property. But, insofar as the property has not been sold, the assessment is an estimate of the market value by the local tax assessor. Property tax assessments are, at best, approximate valuations of a property's market value. Nevertheless, property assessment is the basis for levying the tax rate, which, multiplied by the assessed value, determines the annual tax bill for the property owner. A homeowner whose house is assessed at $100,000 with a tax rate of $3.00 per $100 assessed value would pay a tax of $3,000 or 3 percent of the property's value. Similar houses in the community may be assessed for more or less, depending on market conditions. Thus, property taxes on similar private residential homes could vary markedly. To prevent this unfairness, cities, towns, and municipalities undergo periodic reevaluations to bring all property values up to current "market" values.

Even if we assume that all property assessments are indeed an accurate reflection of market values, the property tax is still unfair! Property does not pay taxes, but people do from their income or savings. Let's examine the hypothetical $100,000 house cited above. This house has been constructed in a particular neighborhood so that several different types of owners currently live in them. Let's see the impact of the property tax on these families.

In one house, a couple earning $80,000 resides with their two school-aged children. If the property tax is $4,000 this family pays 5 percent of its income in taxes to the town for schools, police, roads, sewers, etc. In another house, a retired couple with a yearly income of $40,000 pays 10 percent of its annual earnings for property taxes. Adjacent to the retirees is a childless couple earning $100,000. This $4,000 property tax translates into a 4 percent tax on their income. In still another house a couple earning $56,000 with four children, all in private or religious schools pays nearly 7.5 percent of their income in property taxes. In all instances, the tax is the same— $4,000—but the incidence is markedly different and the benefits received are quite unequal.

Most property taxes are used to fund the local public school system. In our hypothetical example, the cost per student is $3,000 per year. The benefits are received by the families whose children attend the public schools. The family with two children in the schools receives $6,000 of educational benefits for $4,000 in property taxes. The other families receive police and fire protection, street repair, garbage collection, etc., but do not receive any educational services because they either have no children or their children do not attend the public schools. This is grossly unfair. Yet, proponents of property taxes to fund schools cite the "community value" of an educated population. Thus all homeowners should share in the costs of public education. In addition, other proponents of tax-supported public education assert that a community's residential real estate values are a reflection of the quality of its school system. There is merit in this argument if you have school-aged children. In other words, if a community pours money into the school system and the schools do a fine job of educating children, the town will be an attractive place to raise a family. The demand for living in the town will thus be translated into higher housing prices as families bid up the right to live in the community. So, one possible explanation of a town's high housing values is the quality of its public educational services. But, if the town's schools are not the primary motive for living in the town, some families then will find the taxes a substantial burden.

For example, both the retired couple who may have been living in the town for many years and whose children moved away decades ago and the childless couple who recently moved into town, desire to live here despite the tax burden, because they find other amenities, such as climate, closeness to family and friends, proximity to metropolitan areas and work, etc., attractive. Nevertheless, at the local level we clearly see a phenomenon that occurs throughout American society because of the tax system, cross-subsidization. That is, families pay the property tax and receive no direct benefits while other families receive more benefits than they pay for. In our hypothetical community the family with four children attending private and/or religious schools is treated quite unfairly. This family pays for the support of the public schools with its taxes and then pays to educate the children in an educational environment it believes is best. How can anyone support this arrangement?

To argue that property taxes must be imposed to fund public schools because an educated population is in society's interests is a fallacious proposition. First, society's interest is a nebulous concept. Every family raising children should have an interest in educating its children. The responsibility of each family—single or two parent household (How's that for political correctness!)—is to raise its children to be responsible human beings and to provide each child with the necessities of life, including an education. Education could occur at home, in a structured classroom, or in any other setting the parents think is best for their children. But, if we accept the premise that it is society's responsibility to educate children, then educational resources will be allocated by the political process, i.e., tax-and-spend.

Second, if property taxes must be imposed to fund public education because society benefits from an educated population, the logic of this assertion is untenable. "Society" also benefits (let's take this argument to its logical conclusion) from a well-fed, well-dressed, well-housed population. If people need nutritious diets, sufficient clothing, adequate housing, and minimum health care, then taxes should raise the money so government can provide these goods and services to the American people. If so, then the proponents of public education must also advocate complete socialism in order for the people to have all the necessities of life! Of course, no one openly advocates complete socialism for America, but elements of socialism nevertheless have been implemented in the country in a piecemeal fashion, one slice at a time. Public education via property and other taxes is just another slice of the socialist "baloney" being fed to the American people in the name of equity, justice, and the public interest.

Commercial Property Taxation

Property taxes lower the value of business property. When real estate taxes are first imposed on commercial property, the value of the property will decline because the return to the owner will be reduced. For example, if a property has an income of $100,000 and the return investors seek is 10 percent on similar risk investments, the property will be worth $1,000,000. If taxes are imposed reducing the net income to $50,000 investors seeking a 10 percent return will now only value this property at $500,000, thus causing a substantial loss of capital to the owner that cannot be recouped if the tax is permanent. If the owner sells the property for $500,000, the new owner will have a $50,000 income or a 10 percent return. If taxes are raised again, the capital value of the property will be reduced further.

The essential point is that taxation reduces both the income and wealth of business property owners, especially when it is first implemented. As the market adjusts the value of property to taxation, capital may be reluctant to flow into some or all types of commercial real estate because of the uncertainty of future tax burdens. This will cause a misallocation of resources, particularly of multi-family residential housing that is taxed in some locales twice; once directly with property taxes and secondly, indirectly with rent control. Under rent control, the local government in effect imposes a 100 percent tax on the difference between the controlled rent and the market rent. This "tax" is for all intents and purposes a pure subsidy to the renters who pay the controlled below-market rent. Moreover, the lower capital value of the property translates into a lower assessment and hence lower property taxes, which causes taxes to probably be higher on noncontrolled commercial property and private homes. So, strictly from the perspective of tax incidence, the property tax—and indirect taxes—on commercial property can have a devastating impact on locales. Witness the deteriorating New York City residential housing stock, a result, according to many analysts, of strict rent control for many years.

Many factors cause a decline in both economic activity and the housing stock in communities across the country. Taxing property in some cities puts an enormous burden on remaining homeowners and businesses after corporations, small enterprises, and individuals have relocated to more favorable locations. Why businesses and families have been leaving central cities has been analyzed endlessly, and several reasons are rising labor costs, rising crime rates, deteriorating infrastructure, increasing taxes, etc. This phenomenon, the exodus of business from our central cities, should lay to rest the notion that businesses can pass on higher costs to their customers. If rising costs could be passed on to consumers, businesses not only would not leave locales with higher labor utility or other costs, but they would never go bankrupt since charging higher prices would always cover their increasing costs. In short, costs can never be fully passed on to consumers. Why should a businessman have to wait for higher costs to raise prices? Why shouldn't he raise prices any time he wants and reap all the benefits of price increases?

Sales Taxation

A general sales tax is imposed on goods and/or services provided to consumers. Often some goods—for example, food, clothing, and medicine—are exempt, as well as medical fees and other professional services. Sales taxes bring in substantial revenue for state and local governments because it is a broad-based levy.

As the economy has grown over the decades the sales tax has become a primary source of money for state and local governments. These funds are used to deliver a myriad of services—schools, roads, welfare, health care, etc., to the public. Sales taxation, nevertheless, is not a new phenomenon in the government's assault on taxpayers. The sales tax had been used in the colonies sporadically, but it wasn't until the twentieth century that the need for a broad tax to raise revenue during the Great Depression catapulted the levy into a perma-nent—and increasingly higher—burden on the public. How-ever, a few holdout states, most notably New Hampshire, still do not have a sales tax, undoubtedly a legacy of their anti-tax heritage embraced either during the colonial period or their early statehood's existence.

The sales tax is paid by consumers according to con-ventional thinking. After all, assert most economists, a sales tax of 5 percent is tacked on the price of an item, let's say a $100 radio, so the cost to the consumer is now $105. This sounds like a reasonable explanation but it overlooks an important factor. Businesses cannot willy-nilly pass on higher costs—in this case a sales tax—to consumers and expect to sell the same amount of goods as they did prior to the introduction of the tax. For example, if the retailer sold 1,000 radios at $100 last year and on the first of January a 5 percent sales tax is introduced, how many radios will the retailer now sell? Prob-ably less than 1,000 units because if the retailer keeps the price at $100 and tacks on $5 to cover the sales tax, some consumers will be unwilling to pay the extra $5. Some consumers, therefore, will reduce their consumption of radios, because the tax has priced them out of the market. The retailer's gross and net income will be reduced. But, if the retailer lowered his price to $95 and charged $4.75 to cover the sales tax, the price of the radio would remain at approximately $100 and then the retailer will have absorbed the sales tax, thereby reducing his income. The market price of the radio, however, could increase to $105, $100 plus $5 tax, if the supply were reduced, thus raising the "market" price to $105. This would cause some consumers to forego the purchase of the radio, hardly a socially beneficial policy. In addition, if producers maintain the $100 price and pass on the sales tax to consumers, some producers may drop out of the market, thus reducing supply, which would cause the new market price for the radio to be $100 plus the $5 sales tax, or $105. But, why would a producer willingly forego sales to accommodate the government's tax policy? Either way, a sales tax harms both consumers who may pay a higher price and retailers who may sell a lower supply of the product. A recent example of how a federal sales tax (dubbed the luxury tax) lowered consumption and de-stroyed jobs, occurred in the past few years in states like New Jersey. The 10 percent tax on boats, coupled with the early 1990s recession, drove many firms into bankruptcy and caused unemployment for hundreds of workers earning $20–$50,000. This episode should disabuse policymakers in Washington that taxes do not have major negative impacts on both produc-tion and employment.

Another effect of a sales tax is the shopping behavior of consumers. The highway congestion in northern New Jersey on Saturday, with shoppers from New York, is a testimony to how shoppers behave toward a high sales tax—8.25 percent in New York City versus 6 percent in New Jersey (no sales tax on clothing). New York shoppers would have no incentive to travel to New Jersey if merchants in the Big Apple lowered their prices to absorb the tax. To the extent merchants try to "pass on" the tax, many shoppers will take their dollars elsewhere.

The reduction, therefore, of gross and net income will tend to lower the retailer's demand for radios from the wholesaler and manufacturer. They, in turn, will have to reduce their bids for both labor and material in order to keep costs in line with final product prices. The sales tax therefore lowers the incomes of both labor and owners of the original factors of production. In the final analysis, the sales tax is an income tax on workers and the owners of productive factors, land, warehouses, factories, raw materials, etc. Proponents of sales taxation unwittingly (let's give them the benefit of the doubt) harm the very people they presumably want to help with their tax-and-spend policies, the working poor, low—and middle—income workers, and small business owners. The best way to help these people is to abolish the sales tax so they can earn their full income in the marketplace.

Consumption Tax

A tax on consumption is essentially a levy on the amount an individual or family spends on consuming goods and services during the year. The tax could be collected when an individual calculates his gross income minus any savings (purchases of stock, bonds, etc.) made during the year plus any sales of capital assets not reinvested. For example, an individual who earns $30,000, saves $5,000, and sells bonds for $1,000 would be taxed on $26,000, the amount spent on consumption. There are numerous problems with this method of taxation; namely, are mortgage payments savings or consumption? At first glance, a mortgage payment is both, "consuming" part of the house and a form of "saving" by paying off part of the mortgage. Individuals with large mortgages, therefore, would be "saving" more than families

with small mortgages or renters. A consumption tax, therefore, could induce higher income families to buy large houses
as a tax shelter. In addition, what should the consumption tax
rate be? If it is relatively high, low-income people will pay a
substantial proportion of their income to Uncle Sam because
they consume virtually all their income. Even with exemptions for food and shelter or a high threshold, that is, no tax on
say the first $10–$15,000 of income, a consumption tax would
still be with us, violating our privacy, etc., etc., etc.

    Fortunately, a consumption tax has never been imple-
mented in the United States. Primarily, it has been considered
a regressive tax, that is, it falls more heavily on poor and low-
income families inasmuch as these groups spend most of their
income on consumption. In addition, the federal tax code has
promoted consumption instead of savings, a legacy of
Keynesian, demand-side management of the economy. The
Keynesian theory, in summary, asserts that the economy is
sound if consumption remains "high," so a tax on consumption
would tend to dampen consumer spending and set off a
recessionary period, high unemployment, lower output, etc.
Thus, under the influence of Keynesian economic advisers for
the past half century, U.S. presidents have not recommended
a national consumption tax. But, this may change in the future.
Several articles have appeared in the press including, "Is a
Consumption Tax Coming?" (*Investor Business Daily* 2 October 1992) and "Consumption Tax Can Bring Back Thrifty
Americans" (*Wall Street Journal*, 7 October 1992.) The public
is being readied for a new tax in the 1990s. You can bet the
ranch on it! As we saw with the introduction of the income tax
in 1913, tariffs were initially lowered then raised to pre-
income tax level in the 1920s. If a consumption tax is imposed
and income taxes are lowered, the latter taxes will be raised in
the future—guaranteed. History is a wonderful teacher. Public officials hate to give up revenue. They hate to keep their

hands off the people's wallets and pocketbooks. The great tax increase of the 1990s is in the making . . . unless the public embraces at least some of the proposals in *Tax-Free 2000.*

    A consumption tax, in the final analysis, is nothing more than a disguised income tax. If an individual spends all his income then a consumption tax is equivalent to an income tax, inasmuch as consumption equals income. Moreover, a tax on consumption is supposed to shift people's expenditures toward investment rather than consumption so the nation's savings increase, thereby promoting economic growth. This thinking is a form of central planning.

    Taxing consumption instead of income could raise savings. The chart below demonstrates what could happen if a consumption tax replaced the income tax. A 10 percent average income tax is assumed in order to simplify the evaluations. (State and local taxes are ignored for the time being.) For example, an individual earning $3,000 per month will pay $300 to the IRS, spend $2,430, and save $270. This hypothetical individual consumes 90 percent of his after-tax income and saves 10 percent. If the income tax is replaced with a 10 percent consumption tax, the taxpayer would pay less tax ($250), consume more ($2,475), and save more ($275). From a free-market perspective, a 10 percent consumption tax is better than a 10 percent income tax because the individual has more control over his income. In reality, a 10 percent consumption tax is nothing more than an 8.33 percent income tax.

    If the federal government wanted to collect the same amount of tax ($300), the consumption tax would have to be 12.38 percent.

Table 1

Impact of Consumption Tax on Income

Gross Income	Tax	Net Income	Savings
$3,000	$300*	$2,430	$270
$3,000	$250+	$2,475	$275
$3,000	$300•	$2,430	$270
$3,000	$0	$2,700	$300

*10% income tax
+10% consumption tax
• 12.38 consumption tax

Proponents of a consumption tax, however, argue that eliminating taxes on interest, dividends, and capital gains would increase savings substantially. Maybe. Savings would increase if people shift some of their income from consumption to investment. This will occur if people's time preferences change, that is, they forego present consumption (spending today) for savings (greater consumption in the future).

A consumption tax could influence people's time preferences but there is no guarantee that people will increase their savings markedly because savings are untaxed.

Savings, however, can only increase at the expense of consumption. And, the individual may, in fact, not increase his savings if a consumption tax replaces the income tax. People may want to maintain their current living standard, therefore, they may continue to consume at the same level. Moreover, why should the government use taxation to manipulate consumption and savings in society? In other words, should the government's tax policies promote or discourage one kind of activity—savings—at the expense of another, consumption? Shouldn't consumption and savings be based upon the people's voluntary preferences? In short, shouldn't the government remain neutral in the allocation of resources and leave people alone to decide how much they want to consume and save?

Finally, Table 1 demonstrates that a tax-free society could achieve the optimal level of both consumption and savings. The central planners in Washington should take note. They are lowering living standards for all taxpayers, undermining future living standards, and destroying jobs with taxation. But, this may be too much for the ruling elite to comprehend. Or, maybe they do comprehend the negative consequences of taxation and really want to hurt the American economy. In either case, the Washington establishment is harming the American people's standard of living and the sooner the public demands radical change, the sooner the American economy will experience sustainable prosperity and not be faced with a choice of evils.

A final note. Some analysts have suggested the United States adopt a European-style value-added tax or V.A.T. This is a tax on the value added at each stage of the production process from processing raw materials to selling goods at retail establishments. This tax would raise substantial revenues in addition to the revenue raised by the income tax. In the final analysis, a V.A.T. is a comprehensive national sales tax. The U.S. economy needs a V.A.T. like it needs another epidemic. A V.A.T. is a paperwork nightmare. Each business would have to collect incredible amounts of information to determine the cost of the inputs and the value of the outputs and then determine the tax owed on the value added by its operations. A mountain of paper would be required to record all the transactions in our $6 trillion economy. Think of all the trees that would have to be cut to meet this tax. Where are all the environmentalists when they are really needed? Forget the V.A.T!

Summary

All the taxes reviewed above lower the people's standard of living both in the present and in the future, cause resources to be allocated differently than the market (the public) wants, and increases governmental power over the citizens' lives. Taxes put enormous resources into the hands of elected and nonelected officials alike so they can behave like feudal lords, funnelling monies to favored groups and individuals in the name of helping society. If anyone says they are going to make life better in the United States or in your community by taxing the people, ask them one question: If the government is going to spend money by first taking money from the people, how will the public benefit since they will be made poorer? If the answer is incoherent, which it will be, then ask another question: If the government is going to spend money on programs the people really want, why not let people spend their income in their own communities directly, thereby eliminating the federal, state, and municipal tax collection bureaucracies and the overpaid bureaucrats who implement these programs? In other words, if government spending really reflects the public's choices, let's implement these programs voluntarily. The fact that the public's choices would indeed be different from what government spends is not surprising, as five thousand years of history has shown. Taxation as well as borrowing makes substantial government spending possible. That taxation causes continuous harm to the public is indisputable. In the next chapter, we will examine how government spending, the flip side of taxation, impacts the economy.

4

Local Services, Taxes,
and User Fees

A society that lets the government provide goods and services that can be supplied by private business is dabbling in socialism. Since socialism doesn't work, why should we think that semi-socialism will work?

--Susan Lee

Human beings need food, clothing, and shelter. To obtain these goods beyond the subsistence level, humans must be educated about the world they live in. They must acquire knowledge about science and mathematics in order to make it possible to live in villages, towns, and cities, the essence of civilization. Instead of roaming the planet to obtain the meager subsistence nature has to offer, human beings have organized communities for protection against both the elements and aggressive neighbors, thus enjoying the benefits of technology, production, and the division of labor. With a community serving as a home base, trade could develop with individuals located in remote areas. The goods produced locally could be exchanged for other goods or money in other regions or foreign countries.

People exchanged the fruits of their labor for goods and services they wanted. Government provision of goods and services, usually in the form of a monopoly supplying some common products to the people, such as olive oil, salt, etc., was instituted not because the masses clamored for socialism, but as a means for the state to reap huge revenues. In short, socialism was implemented to capture enormous profits for the emperor or king at the expense of the people. If the government didn't have a monopoly it sometimes gave a private firm the exclusive right to produceor distribute a product in exchange for a portion of the profits—a business–government partnership known as state capitalism. This is in contrast to *laissez-faire* capitalism, where no laws restrict the production or distribution of a product; in short, *laissez-faire* is the only genuine "level playing field" in society.

The free market provides the greatest amount of goods the people want because of the division of labor and international specialization produce the greatest output of goods and services. Today, however, we have returned to an earlier age with a slight twist. In bygone eras, government intervened to enrich the monarch and its ruling elite, while the poor masses were supposed to obey and pay. There was no pretense that the state's policies were for the benefit of the people. Currently, policymakers and their supporters outside government have invoked one of the great *non sequiturs* of all time.

> People need (fill in the blank), therefore the government should
> have a program to meet the public's needs, wants, desires.

Historically, every service the government offers has been provided by both the profit and nonprofit sectors. Yet, many—if not most—Americans believe government should continue to provide numerous services which nongovernmental organizations could or should not deliver. Creeping socialism, therefore, has been America's best kept secret, and has accelerated in recent years, in spite of socialism's oppressive history and its massive failures in this century. Nevertheless, the American people will reverse this process—the march toward complete socialism—either out of necessity as the Russians are doing, or out of disgust after realizing where we are headed as a nation if we continue to travel on this road. Hopefully, they will choose the latter approach otherwise resurrecting a free-market economy from the ashes of collectivism could be very painful, as the Russian people are finding out, especially if the market reforms are not done swiftly and the remnants of collectivism are not totally dismantled.

Creeping socialism has been manifested in many areas. In this chapter, we will focus on the services local governments deliver, even if some or a substantial amount of federal dollars are used to pay for the programs.

We will argue, and the evidence will show, that the public sector cannot deliver services better than the private sector. If it could, England would still be a welfare state and Sweden would not be reforming.

Education

Education is big business. Public education expenditures (K-12) total approximately $200 billion. With so many dollars at stake, it is no surprise that any major reforms, let alone complete privatization, will be difficult to achieve. Nonetheless, change is coming because of financial, political, and social pressures.

Public schools were established in the colonial period "to encourage learning in general and religious study in particular."[1] In the nineteenth century, the drive for public education increased dramatically. State constitutions usually incorporated a clause establishing a public school system. In New Jersey, for example, Article VIII, Section IV, Paragraph 1 reads:

> The Legislature shall provide for the maintenance and support of a thorough and efficient system of free public schools for the instruction of all children in the State between the ages of five and eighteen years.

Needless to say, "free" public schools is impossible. All goods and services are relatively scarce and therefore not costless. Someone has to pay for the schools. The New Jersey Constitution's omission on how schools are to be funded resulted in a recent court case challenging the reliance on property taxes to fund public education. The New Jersey Supreme Court ordered the state to increase aid for cities that had been "shortchanged," thus violating the constitutional mandate regarding education. Governor Florio increased spending by nearly $300 million to comply with the court's ruling, even though the constitution does not mention "equal spending," but only a "thorough and efficient system." State aid to affluent districts were cut, causing suburban districts to vigorously complain about their budgets being shortchanged.

According to the language of the paragraph cited above, funding for education should be strictly a state responsibility and not a local function. Local taxes should be abolished and a statewide tax substituted to support public education. This is not an endorsement of public education or statewide taxes but an acknowledgment of a possible interpretation of New Jersey's state constitution.

Public education, meanwhile, invariably leads to conflict, not only in New Jersey but throughout the country. The conflict in New Jersey arose because of the ambiguity of the state constitution, which places in the government's hands a crucial service that could (and should) be provided by the private sector. If the argument that the military is too important to be left to the generals is true, then education is also too important to be left to government bureaucracies.

Educational services can be delivered in several ways: public education with parental choice of schools in the system, public education with parental choice of schools in either public or private schools, home schooling, private education with government assistance, or totally private education with no government assistance. Currently, education is delivered through a combination of public and private schools. Which system should deliver education services will be discussed in Chapter 7, but in keeping with the theme of this book, private schools--both profit and nonprofit-- should replace the public school system for a variety of reasons.

Virtually no one believes the current no-choice public education system is ideal. Even many members of the educational establishment have endorsed public school choice as a welcome reform. David Osborne and Ted Gaebler in *Reinventing Government: How the Entrepreneurial Spirit is Transforming the Public Sector* cite the successful experiments in such diverse areas as District 4 in Manhattan, and Minnesota, as evidence that "a carefully crafted choice-managed competition" can improve student performance in the public schools. The reported increase in student performance within a public school choice environment is a welcome benefit to students, parents, teachers and administrators. However, is public choice the optimal educational system for children?

Even if a public school system allows parents to choose their children's schools, parents and their children are still being shortchanged. Some critics of the public education monopoly want to allow parents to obtain a voucher from the public schools or local governmental body to purchase education in a nongovernmental school. After all, parents pay taxes—forced extractions—the argument goes, and they should have the right to send their children to schools in the non-public sector that meet their criteria for a sound education. Opponents of vouchers—using "government" money to purchase private education—claim this is "undemocratic," "unconstitutional," and even possibly "racist." Let's examine these criticisms.

Public education is supposed to be the great equalizer in America, children from all socioeconomic backgrounds learning the virtues of democracy, freedom, etc., in the great melting pot, the United States. America's strength, therefore, is children learning about the virtues of citizenship and becoming responsible, literate individuals. This idealized image of public schools does not conform with the facts. A primary reason for the establishment of public schools was to eliminate the diversity of America's immigrants, not encourage it, and mold them into "subordination and obedience" to the state. If the government is providing "free" education to children, isn't the state then a wonderful institution that should be supported in order to bring more benefits to the people? The enactment of compulsory attendance laws revealed that education was secondary to both the educational establishment and public officials. Removing children from both work and the home, even though parents needed either the income or wanted to educate their children about their values, underscores the assertion that public education has been used as a measure to control the population. As cynical as the above sounds, think about this proposition: if education is a valuable service, then why don't parents have the right to determine the kind of education they want for their children? Otherwise, we fall into the *non sequitur* trap: Education is wanted, needed, etc., therefore the government should provide it. Don't parents obtain food, clothing, and medical care for their children without the hand of the state interfering? Why should education be any different?

Vouchers are not "undemocratic" because parents would, in effect, be using their own money, which have become "tax dollars," to purchase educational services in a non-governmental institution. In short, parents would be "reclaiming" some of the hard-earned money to meet their children's educational needs. How can this be construed as "undemocratic"? Vouchers seem more like justice, the right of parents to educate their children with a portion of their tax dollars. The government has no money except what it appropriates from the citizenry, so to decry vouchers as a "giveaway" to parents is to practice a new religion—secular statism—the belief that 100 percent of an individual's income belongs to the state and what an individual keeps is a grant or subsidy from the government. This idea is a perversion of freedom and genuine democracy.

Some free-market proponents criticize vouchers for use in private schools. They believe that with "government" dollars comes governmental control over both private and nondenominational religious schools. This is a valid point. Inevitably, "government dollars" means governmental control over curriculum, teaching qualifications, and racial, ethnic, and gender balance. These interferences become paramount to bureaucrats rather than teaching and learning. In short, schools have become laboratories for sociologists, philosophers, public officials, political scientists, et. al., to construct a mini-world according to the latest social fad.

As far as the unconstitutionality of vouchers is concerned, it seems that any policy that hints of "supporting" religion is considered *ipso facto* unconstitutional. But, the broader issue is ignored. Parents are coerced into supporting public education and some parents may believe the ideas taught in the schools are abhorrent to their value systems. In short, proponents of public education and opponents of vouchers are hypocritical. They renounce the use of vouchers for religious-oriented schools, but demand parents pay for the upkeep of public education, which may be criticizing or denigrating their belief systems. Hence, the inevitable conflict arises between parents who want to educate their children in a school that practices their religious beliefs and the government which says okay, but you cannot use taxpayers' dollars, even your own. Don't both the educational and political establishment realize the anger and frustration they are fomenting with their ideology, strengthening the state at all costs, even if social unrest occurs? Compassion and humane concern for their fellow citizens who differ from the established philosophy apparently should not be tolerated when it comes to delivering educational services. Monopolists always sing the same tune: we know what is best for you so keep quiet and pay up.

If the proponents of public education cannot win the undemocratic and unconstitutional argument against vouchers, there is the old standby—racism. Won't vouchers exclude minorities from some private schools and therefore bring us segregation? First, the civil rights statutes prohibit discrimination. Second, private and parochial schools have educational philosophies which may not be compatible with minority parents, so these schools would be unattractive anyway under a voucher system. What's the fuss then? Racism is a "red herring" to scare public officials from approving a voucher system, lest they be tagged racists. Racism has thus replaced "McCarthyism" as an effective smear to silence one's opponents in today's political battles.

Although there hasn't been a more contentious issue in the United States than forced integration of the public school and other facilities, ironically, with the discovery of racial and ethnic pride over the past several decades, some minorities want to segregate themselves! What is a white liberal to do? If integration has been the goal because minorities would obtain better education or "equal" treatment in the marketplace in a non-discriminatory society, what policies should be implemented that would allow minorities to voluntarily segregate themselves? Under the equal protection clause of the U.S. Constitution, doesn't it seem fair that any group—racial, ethnic, gender, religious, etc.—has the right, the inalienable right, to form an association with people who share a common characteristic? If so, then private schools, religious or nonreligious, should be free to choose the qualifications of their students without governmental interference. Some schools may indeed exclude people because they fail to meet a specific characteristic but this occurs in all walks of life, not just schools, e.g., dating, marriage, friendship, and patronizing shops. (Only job and housing discrimination are illegal. In other activities, people can discriminate to their hearts' content without breaking the law!)

A humane, and in fact, natural approach to education would be for schools to be established based upon a variety of criteria, e.g., pro-socialism, pro-free market, pro (fill in), Christian, non-Christian, atheistic, new world order, old world order, segregated, integrated, etc. In short, a true melting pot of ideas, philosophies, and orientations, that characterizes America would flourish in schools if the government would loosen its grip on the people's choices. Instead, conflict continues because of a virtual government monopoly over education. Government monopolies, in the long run, are ineffective, and we are in the long run.

In the final analysis, vouchers are unnecessary. Transforming the public schools into nonprofit or profit-making institutions would eliminate such controversial issues as prayer in schools, condom distribution, and other controversial ideas. Parents who want prayers in public schools are forbidden by law to have their wishes fulfilled. Parents who do not want condoms distributed to their children are prevented from exercising their parental rights. Mandated sex education classes may violate some parents' value system. As more programs are mandated in the public schools or are prohibited from being exercised there, parental responsibility is diminished and conflict ensues. In other words, public schools fail to meet the need of all their consumers. How many private businesses exist that fail to meet their customers' needs?

Home schooling has boomed in recent years because parents have been unhappy with the education establishment. Estimates of children being taught at home range from 500,000 to more than 1 million. Whatever the exact number, "some observers believe that home schooling will be a major trend in American education, reflecting the broader social trends of self-help as opposed to reliance on institutions to deliver services."[2] Needless to say, the education establishment has condemned home schooling because it believes it is inadequate to meet the needs of children. In fact, the National Association of Elementary School Principals denounced home schooling in a resolution which states, among other things, home schooling "may be provided by non-certified and unqualified persons." For thousands of years parents have been raising their children, including teaching them the 3Rs and other subjects, yet today's parents who are much more educated than their prehistoric, ancient, or medieval ancestors are unqualified to teach their children! In essence, children must be taught by an education elite or they may be dumb forever. Well, based on the skills of many high school students graduating today, could home schooling do any worse in educating them? In fact, home schooling may be just what some students need—individual attention and close supervision.

Welfare

Mention welfare in a family gathering or in a group of friends or colleagues and someone's blood pressure is bound to head for the stratosphere. That's how emotional this issue has become. Welfare can be discussed objectively so appropriate public policies can be formulated that would reduce the dependency of families and individuals on the dole—a supposed goal of public officials and most academes. We will examine welfare policies and discuss the impact on people dependent upon substantial government subsidies for their living expenses.

We have reached a critical juncture in the history of welfare in the United States. We now have an opportunity to do something, once and for all, about the "welfare mess." Nobody, absolutely nobody—not the recipients, not the case workers, administrators, government officials, taxpayers—a unanimous consensus, thinks the current welfare system is doing a good job. The "system" is demeaning, fostering corruption, breaking up families, and condoning out-of-wedlock births; in brief, it is anti-human.

From what began as a modest program under Franklin Roosevelt's administration, Aid to Families with Dependent Children (AFDC) had approximately 13.5 million recipients including 9.1 million children in 1992, up from 2 million in 1950 and 4 million in 1965. In addition, recipients are eligible for food stamps and receive free medical coverage under Medicaid. Maximum monthly cash benefits and food stamps vary from state to state, with a low of $412 in Mississippi to $1,184 in Alaska.

The federal government, meanwhile, defines a poverty level of income for three people as $940 a month. Clearly, being on welfare is not exactly living the "good" life. Nevertheless, with nearly five percent of the population on welfare, and for some families a virtual permanent existence, the welfare system epitomizes a failed social policy of enormous proportions. The average time spent on welfare for first-time recipients is six-and-one-half years, while nearly a quarter of the families receiving AFDC have been on welfare for ten years or more.[3] How is it possible that a modest program aimed at helping widows and orphans became a way of life for so many women with out-of-wedlock children?

The short, fundamental answer to swelling welfare rolls can be summed up in one word: entitlement. The social revolution of the 1960s elevated government welfare spending into a "right." No longer was welfare considered a temporary safety net bridging employment; it became a program to sustain people for as long as they wanted to receive public assistance. Welfare has been transformed from a helping hand into "a way of life." Armed with anti-poverty and "welfare rights" lawyers, recipients have become another interest group intent on preserving—and expanding—their access to taxpayers' dollars. In short, welfare recipients believe as other individuals receiving a government check that these funds are available for distribution among worthy groups and that their plight is just as worthy a cause as the next one. Everyone forgets, however, that before the government disburses this largesse, it must first do a little extraction of its own from taxpayers.

That welfare is seen as a "right" in our society demonstrates that marked philosophical shift in the nation. In the nineteenth century, "welfare" was supplied privately, in keeping with the ideological tenor of the times. Moreover, the poor were not then discarded as proponents of welfare rights would have us believe. Instead, the poor were treated more humanely than in the current system. In the last century, some poor workers received supplemental assistance from private charities; other individuals who were incapable of working were sent to the poorhouse. The rest who refused to work, even though they were capable of doing an honest day of labor, were identified as "paupers" and were considered the dregs of society for their lack of self-responsibility.

The poorhouse allowed people to obtain meager subsistence in exchange for a "controlled" environment. Rather than allowing the poor to consume alcohol, engage in prostitution or promiscuity, the poorhouse did not want its inhabitants to engage in destructive behavior, including out-of-wedlock births.

Workhouses were established "to insure that no person would be without food and shelter for lack of work."[4] Workhouses thus made it possible for individuals to work for their subsistence instead of receiving cash for nothing in exchange. Unlike the current welfare system which grants money, food stamps, subsidized housing, and free medical care to families, the nineteenth century programs were established to instill dignity. Today's poor, in the final analysis, have many of the characteristics of last century's paupers, the so-called undeserving poor who refused to work, whose personal conduct, including drug addiction, alcoholism, and illegitimacy, would not have been tolerated a hundred years ago. Instead, the current welfare system makes it more advantageous to stay on welfare then accept low paying jobs that would allow people to obtain skills in order to move up the economic ladder. Without having the skills that command high incomes, poor people must start at the "bottom" and work themselves up. There is no other method to propel low-income individuals into middle-income individuals overnight. Anyone asserting there is a shortcut to a middle class income for unskilled, uneducated individuals is being disingenuous.

The welfare system's perverse incentives, moreover, perpetuate the unwed mother syndrome because more benefits can be obtained without a father in the household. Government policy, therefore, is culpable. It makes nonwork more attractive than work and it encourages the creation of single mother head of household families, the poorest group in society. In addition, government welfare programs undermine the values that are necessary to escape the "poverty trap," e.g., thriftiness, personal responsibility and punctuality. With such a track record, government welfare deserves to be abolished and welfare recipients need a method to restore their dignity, self-respect, and independence.

Roads, Highways, and Bridges

High-tech is here. Highways and bridges are entering a new era. Instead of a grumpy toll collector taking your money after you have waited endlessly in a congested toll plaza, an automated computerized toll system allows you to whisk by without stopping or even slowing down. Such a system is already in use on some highways around the country, and by the turn of the century it will undoubtedly be the primary method of collecting tolls, user fees, on highways and bridges. The toll will be able to be modified in order to introduce peak and off-peak pricing, a method that will reduce both congestion and pollution, and lowers the need for more roads.

In the meantime, why is the infrastructure in such bad shape, given all the gasoline taxes motorists and truckers have paid over the years? It wasn't always this way. The private sector built most of the country's infrastructure during the nation's first 150 years.[5] With the shift in philosophy in the early twentieth century, local and state governments began to build and operate facilities competing with private sector enterprises. The private companies had to pay taxes while government enterprises were tax-exempt. In addition, the debt issued by government agencies are tax-exempt so interest charges have been lower than similar securities issued by private corporations whose debt holders are taxed on the interest they receive. You don't need a Ph.D. in finance to realize there is no level playing field between government and the private sector. Taxpayers guarantee the government debt, thereby making the projects virtually riskless to government bureaucrats. Thus, unless the project's revenue stream does not cover the debt service, taxpayers will be saddled with higher taxes to make up for any shortfalls. Moreover, if the facility deteriorates, taxpayers are hit with higher taxes for repairs and/or more debt is issued in a vicious circle to pay for government mismanagement. Either way, taxes rise to pay for the government's ineptness.

Although the nation's infrastructure is considered an essential element of our international competitive posture, government—at all levels— has been responsible for developing, constructing, and maintaining these facilities, with predictable results. The reliance on the public sector to move people and goods has resulted in congested roads and bridges and deteriorating facilities. Without pricing facilities according to peak demand periods, bridges, highways, and airports have become more congested than they otherwise would be. Crossing the George Washington Bridge from New Jersey to New York costs $4.00 (or less if you have a commuter book) both during the morning rush period and the wee hours after midnight when there is virtually no one travelling into the city. This is an unsound pricing policy. This "flat" toll system exists in virtually all governmental delivery of services. (The Port Authority of New York and New Jersey which operates the Hudson River crossings and other transportation facilities in the metropolitan area is a quasi-public agency. It is a creature of both states' legislatures). The post office is another example of pricing services on a flat fee basis. Mailing a first class letter to a neighbor costs the same as mailing it to Hawaii, 5,000 miles from the east coast. In other words, "short-haul" users, in effect, subsidize "long-haul" users.

The current pricing system of government facilities is inefficient and should be overhauled in order (1) to bring demand and supply into better balance, and (2) reduce congestion and thus pollution, in the case of roads and highways. But, the desire to "democratize" prices of government-provided services has led to undesirable consequences, even though sound analytical techniques have predicted the results for decades. Public officials have been behind "the curve" on the subject for years but economic reality is giving way to illogical blinders. The costs of constructing new transportation facilities to handle demand is not a viable option for many communities, so by default public administrators are now realizing they have to use the current facilities more efficiently. This means a pricing system that takes into account peak and off-peak demand. Eventually, public officials learn, but in the meantime the people have to suffer commuting to work and businesses have their costs increased because of government mismanagement.

Libraries, Parks, Museums

Virtually every level of government in the country provides cultural and recreational facilities. Communities take pride in their well-stocked libraries, attractive museums, and manicured parks. Many of the country's citizens use these facilities and support the expenditure of tax dollars for their maintenance. However, the use of tax dollars for libraries, parks, museums, and other facilities undermines, again, a sound allocation of resources in society. For some citizens, their use of these facilities is virtually impossible (national parks, for example), limited (libraries and museums), or unwanted (beaches). To extract funds from the people to pay for facilities desired by some or a vast majority of the population is simply unfair. If low- or middle-income people are taxed when their use of these facilities is extremely rare, then their standard of living is adversely affected. As much as these activities are desired by the vast majority of the population, there must be a rational way of allocating these scarce resources, namely a user fee for entrance or an annual, quarterly, or monthly payment system.

When public facilities do charge a fee, and there is still a shortfall to cover operating expenses, governmental subsidies come to the rescue. Fees are in use for numerous goods and services, e.g., newspaper and magazine subscriptions, water use, automobile and home insurance, video rentals, etc. In other words, in order for public officials to know what these facilities are worth to the people, we need to install the price mechanism so a relationship is established between payment made and benefits received. Otherwise, the quality of these public services will deteriorate; for example, witness the cutback on hours in recent years of parks, museums, libraries, etc., because of local, state, or federal budget squeezes. In addition, without a price system in place, officials will be unable to deliver the services to meet consumer demand, a key failure of socialism.

It is not surprising that the public is more unhappy with the delivery of public services than with services in the private sector. In fact, retailers, fast food restaurants, etc., are constantly devising ways to better meet customers' needs. If private businesses do not meet consumer needs, they suffer losses, a signal that they should "get their act together" or go out of business. How many public sector facilities go out of business because they failed to meet the citizens' needs? Instead, they may even get their budgets increased in spite of their poor performance. In the final analysis, which facility is cleaner, safer, and more fun—Disneyworld or the national parks? End of debate. What the country needs, therefore, is a "Disneyization" of public facilities. "Mickey," "Minnie," and "Donald" probably can deliver these services better than public bureaucrats. Besides, they're a lot cuter! Whether these facilities are profit or nonprofit enterprises depends on specific circumstances. But, the idea merits consideration, the complete desocialization of public facilities is an idea whose time has come.

Housing

Everyone needs a roof over his or her head. Shelter is a fundamental want of human beings. But, to leap to the conclusion that government should construct and manage residential housing or regulate privately-owned multi-family units is to apply tortured logic, i.e., the great *non sequitur*: Housing is a valued and needed service, therefore, all levels of government must be involved to ensure decent conditions for the American people. Although the nation's first public housing project was not opened until 1938 on the Lower East Side of Manhattan, the policies of the New Deal set into motion substantial government involvement in the housing sector for the next several decades.

Initially, public housing was intended for middle income tenants, but, as so often happens, poor families began to move in. Soon, welfare recipients became the prime residents of public housing, and with this dramatic demographic change came "a vicious cycle of drugs, crime, teenage pregnancy and welfare dependency."[6] "By the 1950s, public housing was . . . in trouble," according to William Tucker's chronicle of America's housing policies in *The Excluded Americans: Homelessness and Housing Policies*. Tucker's insightful presentation pinpoints the results of the federal government's intervention in the housing market. Urban renewal, the supposed showcase of the federal government's programs, demolished tens of thousands of housing units occupied by poor and low-income families through 1964, over two-thirds of whom were blacks, Puerto Ricans, and other minorities.[7] After the urban riots of the mid- and late-1960s, the Johnson administration and then the Nixon administration assisted in the construction of over 1 million public and private units. By the early 1970s, scandals rocked two of the programs, Sections 235 and 236. The latter "encouraged non-profit groups to build rental housing by offering government mortgage subsidies that lowered their interest rate to one percent," while the former assisted slum dwellers to buy "homes on the private market for as little as $200 down payment. Their mortgages could then be subsidized so that they would pay as little as 20 percent of their income in monthly payments."[8] The 235 program scandal involved "fast buck artists" making shoddy improvements in inner city houses, which were then sold to neighborhood residents at inflated prices. Mortgages made by the Federal Housing Administration were approved by the agency's own inspectors who had accepted bribes for their cooperation. The homeowners walked away from their houses "leaving the FHA to pay off the banks."[9] Eventually, more than 500 people were convicted in one of the nation's greatest housing scandals.

The 236 program ended after the nonprofit sponsors' management revealed the pending bankruptcy of 20 percent of the projects over the next decade. But, more instructive was the realization that poor families constituted only 43 percent of the tenants. Both middle-income and lower-middle-income families became the greatest recipients of rent subsidies under the program instead of the poor. To rectify this situation, the Nixon administration proposed and the Congress passed a new housing bill in 1974 containing a "housing certificate." Not quite a "rent stamp," these "Certificates constitute a 15-year commitment by the government to pay the difference between a tenant's rent and 30 percent of his income. The payment is made to the landlord, not the tenant."[10]

Developers, encouraged by the federal government's virtual guarantee of filling their units with low-income residents, saw a full gravy train to board. In addition, certificates would be issued for tenants in existing housing as well as for rehabilitation of existing housing units. The distribution of these certificates became, you guessed it, political. Lobbying for these certificates intensified during the 1980s, and former Reagan administration officials were paid substantial fees to obtain Section 8 certificates for their clients. These question-able practices, as well as some illegal activities at HUD during the 1980s, led HUD Secretary Jack Kemp to discontinue the program in 1989.

The failure of federal housing programs was captured in the demolition of the Pruitt-Igoe houses, "only fifteen years after they were built because they had become dangerous, vacant and vandalized."[11] No better example of wasting taxpayers' money could be identified than the destruction of housing, a relatively scarce commodity. But, if the dynamit-ing of a public housing project is a powerful image of government's failure to maintain decent premises for poor and low-income families, then regulating a community's housing stock is no less destructive.

Rent control has been as powerful as bombs in destroy-ing multifamily housing in the United States. An excellent overview of New York City's experience with rent control is presented by Jack Richman, a city planner, in *Privatization for New York: Competing for a Better Future.* This collection of essays was prepared for the New York State Senate Advisory Commission on Privatization, chaired by Ronald S. Lauder. In addition to addressing the city's housing situation, the report also examines a variety of issues, focusing on the costly, inefficient provision of services delivered by the municipal government, state agencies, and various authorities.

New York City's fifty-year experience with rent con-trol is one of the country's most appalling examples of eco-nomic regulation run amok. What began as a federal World War II emergency price control measure blossomed into a powerful local wrecking ball of the city's housing stock. According to Richman, rent control has caused thousands of small property owners to lose their life savings, the city to lose hundreds of thousands of apartments to abandonment, and New Yorkers to suffer from a government-created housing shortage.[12] The conclusion is obvious to anyone who has studied microeconomics. Below-market rents reduce the cash flow property owners need to properly maintain their buildings. Inflation and rising property taxes result in insufficient funds for maintenance. Deterioration accelerates, rents are withheld, and a vicious downward spiral plunges a portion of the housing stock into foreclosure and/or abandonment. The city becomes a landlord of last resort. Socialized housing accelerates. More housing is lost because the city doesn't have the funds to maintain the buildings either. Eventually, some apartments are rehabilitated at great cost and the housing stock tends to stabilize, but in the meantime substantial hardship and financial losses occur, especially for the small property owner who may have risked his life savings to purchase the property.

Supposedly, rent control was going to protect the poor from exorbitant rents, instead below-market rents have been a bonanza for rich residents of rent-controlled apartments such as movie stars, corporate executives, Wall Street investment bankers, lawyers and, not surprisingly, local and state elected officials, including, at one time, former Mayor Ed Koch.[13] In fact, rent control actually hurts the poor and lower income families the most because of what is known as being "stranded" in rent-controlled apartments. In other words, many elderly individuals live in large apartments (three, four, or five bedrooms) because it would be much more expensive to rent a one-bedroom apartment under the city's crazy quilt rent regulations. So, single individuals occupy too much space, while large poor and low- and middle-income families occupy one, two, or three bedroom apartments that are deteriorating. Rather than having a rational allocation of living space, rent control diminishes the logical, "natural" mobility of families to apartments that best suit their needs.

In the final analysis, rent control is a 100 percent tax on the difference between the apartment's legally fixed rent and the market rent. In other words, if an apartment in New York could rent for $1,000 a month in a free market but the legal maximum is $700, the tenant receives a $300 subsidy from the government, no questions asked. The property owner receives $300 less than the market rent in effect having this amount taxed 100 percent for the benefit of the tenant only. This is an example of a customized income tax. Where is the American Civil Liberties Union decrying this injustice?

The housing sector epitomizes the inevitable results of both socialism and interventionism in one sector of the economy. No decent human being can be pleased with the government's foray into building or regulating housing, yet some individuals still call for a greater role for government in housing. Blinded by collectivist ideology, the self-styled champions of the poor and lower income groups should be made to (1) attempt to find an apartment in New York City and (2) live in a rent-controlled apartment. Better yet, they should own a rent-controlled building, and see what it is like to have their property confiscated. As one Chinese-American owner of a rent-controlled building concluded after nearly being killed by a tenant who firebombed her building: "In China, when they want to take your property, they just kill you and get it over with . . . Here they torture you first. I think I prefer it the old way."[14] To add insult to injury, the courts refused to evict the tenant or charge him with attempted murder. With the resurrection of free markets in China, Beijing may be safer for property owners than New York!

This is one of many stories recounted by William Tucker, of individuals of modest means who have gone through hell to have their property rights enforced. When the government protects destructors of property instead of owners of property, then civilization is retrogressing. When the courts fail to enforce valid contracts, in effect allowing tenants to avoid paying rent in spite of the property owners' best efforts to improve building conditions, we are on the road to the elimination of private property rights and the end of whatever economic freedoms we currently possess. The challenge for the decade is for the courts to once again be a bastion of enforcing property rights. Otherwise, we might as well hand over all our possessions to the government.

The States and Spending

At the state level, education and welfare are usually the largest government expenditures. Previous comments about these outlays at the local level are even more appropriate at the state level. State taxes (sales, income, etc.) are collected from individuals and businesses and then distributed to counties, cities, towns, and boroughs to pay for public education and welfare services. Strictly from an efficiency criteria, layers of bureaucracy are created to administer these outlays, thereby reducing the funds that would have gone directly to the schools or possible welfare recipients. As a result, both taxes and spending are higher than they otherwise would be to deliver the current level of services. Bureaucracies thus eat up resources that do not go to higher teacher salaries, better equipment in the classroom, or possibly smaller class size. Welfare recipients have to contend with a bureaucratic maze to determine eligibility requirements, benefit levels, and other legal mandates.

State, as opposed to local, administration of both education and welfare cannot be justified on efficiency grounds. Taxpayers and their children in the public schools are short-changed while the administration of welfare has become highly bureaucratized because of all the federal and state regulations that accompany these outlays. Proponents of these programs should therefore call for their decentralization. The fear, which is real, is that communities may abolish public education and/or welfare benefits. This should not be surprising, inasmuch as the support for these programs should come from the community as opposed to mandates from Washington or the state capital.

Should the states continue to "own" and operate parks, museums, beaches, etc.? Fairness dictates that user fees be implemented to cover costs rather than taxpayer subsidies. Until these facilities are privatized, the optimal solution, from the point of view of the non-users, is for users to pay for the expenses of operating these facilities. This would be democracy in action instead of coercing people to pay for services they do not use. To assert that so-called public facilities are for "all the people" is begging the question. Some—or even many—people may not want these facilities and to force them to pay for them is an excellent example of legal plunder.

State colleges and universities share the same characteristics as other public enterprises. They directly benefit a portion of the population, while everyone is taxed to support them. As nonprofit institutions they should be tuition driven and supported by other noncoercive methods, corporate and foundation grants, endowments, fundraisers, etc. This, in short, is a preview of the blueprint outlined in Chapter 7. Our guideline is clear: resources must be allocated to their best use utilizing the market mechanism. Otherwise, political jockeying, influence peddling, intensive lobbying, and eventually economic instability and social disharmony emerge as citizens scramble to protect their interests in the state's spending stream. When the inevitable crisis occurs (the California fiscal crisis of 1992 may be a forerunner for all the states in the 1990s), the people are faced with two fundamental choices— to continue to rely on the public sector to deliver services or to restructure the economy so market solutions can be utilized. As Ross Perot would say, "It's up to the people." It certainly is.

The Federal Leviathan

Understood as a central consolidated power, managing and
directing the various general interests of society, all government is evil . . . The best government is that which governs least.

--John L. O'Sullivan

Social Security and national defense are the federal
government's two greatest expenditures. Medicare/Medicaid
expenditures come in a not-too-distant third. In the proposed
1995 federal budget, which begins on 1 October 1994, Social
Security may reach $335 billion, the military is budgeted for
$271 billion, and Medicare/Medicaid could account for $250
billion of taxpayers' money. These three categories ($961
billion) would account for roughly two-thirds of all federal
spending in fiscal 1995, $1.52 trillion dollars. While per capita
federal spending is approximately $6,000, "the federal gov-
ernment spends more than $11,000 per elderly, $13,000 per
poor household, more than $13,000 per farm worker, and more
than $1,000 per veteran in the U.S."[1] In short, federal spending
is becoming more and more "targeted" to specific groups of
Americans. It is, therefore, not surprising that there is a
growing feeling among Americans that they are getting less
and less for their federal taxes.

With all federal taxes gobbling up approximately 28
percent of an average American's budget in 1993, a fundamental reassessment of the federal government's role in our
society is underway in many households. Notwithstanding the
rhetoric of public officials and academics who believe the
federal government should spend (now it is called "invest")

more, polls indicate Americans believe about one-half of their
tax dollars are being wasted. Why then do the masses and the
ruling elite and their supporters-apologists have different
perceptions about federal spending? Let's look at the three
major federal government spending programs to uncover how
these perceptions affect America's financial dilemma, the
acceleration of government spending, the annual mega-defi-
cit, the federal budget and the $4 trillion-plus national debt.

National Defense

National defense is considered the quintessential "collective good," that is, a service that cannot exclude anyone
from the benefits, even if some individuals do not pay for it, the
so-called "free-ride." The government, therefore, is supposed
to step in, supply the service, and tax the people to pay for it.
This is the economic justification for government provision of
national defense and other so-called public goods. Another
compelling reason for having a single defense agency guard
the country from attack is because individually we cannot
muster sufficient resources to repel an attack from foreign
enemies. But collectively, like an insurance pool, the government can obtain money from every citizen through taxation to
purchase the necessary military equipment, hire a sufficient
number of soldiers, sailors, and pilots to guard and, if necessary, to fight if an attack is made against our nation. At a
minimum, the country needs a military force to safeguard the
people from potential aggressors. The issues that still need to
be resolved, however, are (1) How large should the military
be? (2) What is the national security of the United States and
how is it to be protected? (3) How should military expenditures
be funded? The first two questions will be examined in this
chapter while the last query will be addressed in chapter 7.

The Preamble to the U.S. Constitution states, "We the people" . . . will . . ."provide for the common defence *(sic)* . . ." Constitutionally, the United States government is authorized to protect the nation from foreign aggressors. No one but dedicated pacifists object, therefore, to the country having a military force. Furthermore, Article I, Section 8, Paragraph I, gives Congress the power "to lay and collect taxes, duties, imposts, and excises, to pay . . . for the common defence . . . of the United States." Having laid the foundation for establishing a national defense agency, the United States government must exercise its powers judiciously so that the citizens are not taxed—and our forces sent to die—to support military adventurism overseas. In short, the military must be used to "protect and defend" the territorial integrity of the United States; otherwise, the danger is too great, too tempting, for the nation's rulers to use force for purposes other than justifiable military actions. World history, as we examined in Chapter 2, has been a series of episodes in which nations have attempted to expand aggressively beyond their borders. Nations have used their military strength to plunder other nations or have entered into alliances to jointly plunder their neighbors. In all cases, the people have paid dearly with their wealth and blood. Peaceful coexistence has been one of mankind's elusive goals since the beginning of time, but the world may be on the threshold of a sustained period of peace, if certain fundamental policy changes are implemented in the United States as well as in the rest of the world.

With the end of the Cold War, the United States is the world's only military superpower. The threat from the East, if not totally eliminated, is greatly diminished. Russia still has a substantial number of missiles and nuclear weapons, but unless the leaders of the former Soviet Union are suicidal, which they do not appear to be, they will continue to dismantle their nuclear arsenal. One obvious concern for the U.S. and our allies is the sale of Russia's nuclear weapons to other nations. Nuclear proliferation is a destabilizing military and political phenomenon. The less nuclear weapons in the world the better, because they are weapons of mass destruction, which means the masses die quickly instead of dying during several years of battle. The United States therefore should take the lead in undertaking a global nuclear disarmament campaign, not unilaterally, but a negotiated drawdown of nuclear weapons with all nations who have these weapons.

The United States' nuclear umbrella, which may have been appropriate during the Cold War, serves no strategic purpose in the post–Soviet Union era. Rebuilding domestic economics, both here and abroad, must be the first priority within a context of international stability. Preparing for war does not only undermine economic development, it makes the possibility of war greater. The United States not only fought two wars in the post–World War II period in Korea and Vietnam, which some analysts felt were dubious military ventures, but the recent Gulf War demonstrated that the rationale for U.S.-led intervention was built, according to some critics, on the sand the war was fought on. Whether the costs of each military operation was justified on strategic and national security interests can be debated endlessly. But, if U.S. foreign policy continues to be based on the premise that military force is justified even though the territorial integrity of our country is not in jeopardy, then America's sons and daughters will, unfortunately, die overseas in some dubious future intervention. Developing a coherent, defensive military strategy, then, is essential to ensuring peace, because a potential aggressor must know the people are united in a common bond, protecting the country from attack.

Military expenditures are projected to decline in the 1990s, reflecting the reality of a less hostile world after the dissolution of the Soviet Empire. By 1998, military expenditures may decline to $257 billion or lower, depending on congressional authorizations. The $257 billion figure was projected by President Clinton in the 1995 budget submitted to Congress in February 1994. In President Clinton's discussion of the nation's security needs, he cites the new reality in the post–Soviet Union era and concludes that "the health of the American economy and its competitiveness in a healthy global economy" is a major priority.[2] The Clinton administration believes that more government intervention in the economy is necessary because of increased global competition for U. S. firms. In short, the "Clintonites" assert that they know what trade relationships must be established for U. S. companies to prosper internationally. Although the Clinton officials do not come right out and say it, they believe they can take America to the "Promised Land" by exercising power in Washington.

The United States government accepted an unprecedented role in the post–World War II era, to build and maintain a mighty military force to offset the growing power of the Soviet Union. Clearly, the costs of the military had—and are still having—a substantial impact on the economy. In fact, David Stockman, former member of Congress and director of the Office of Management and Budget under President Reagan, said in 1991: "The 1980s turned out to be a race between the United States and the Soviet Union to see which could achieve fiscal bankruptcy first, and the Soviets won—by a hair."[3] Stockman believes that the deficit is no longer a threat to the economy because of the slowdown in military spending.

Excessive military expenditures always pose a problem for the economy, namely, the opportunity cost of producing weapons—the reduction in the output of both consumer and producer goods, and the shifting of research and development money from civilian uses to military applications. Wasteful and/or excessive military expenditures lower the output of goods and services available to the public, depriving the people of a greater supply of consumer goods and hence lower prices. Consumers thus lose two ways, lower supply of goods and higher prices. This phenomenon was clearly evident in the former Soviet Union. What consumer goods were available could be found on the black market at much higher prices than in the legal markets. With real military spending scheduled to decline during the rest of the decade, then the American people will be the beneficiaries of more resources flowing to the civilian sector instead of industrial enterprises producing military equipment. In addition, a lower demand for military personnel will mean more employees available to meet various needs in the economy, e.g., education, retraining, day care, elder care, health care, drug counselling, etc. Lower military spending also means a transition for some corporations and their employees who have depended on contracts for their revenue and salaries. Transitions can be painful periods. We will discuss how to have as painless a transition as possible in Chapter 8.

Less military spending is a blessing for the economy. But, how much should the military spend to defend the country? And, what constitutes the national security interests of the United States? These issues need to be resolved for the country's economic health and world peace. One proposition that needs to be discussed is the placement of U.S. troops overseas. Even if the U.S. military is "invited" by a foreign country to station troops overseas, should the U.S. accept? Is it in the American people's interests to have its forces exposed to regional conflict and become involved in these disputes? If we accept the premise then that U.S. military should not intervene overseas, even if our government's intentions are pure and noble, what should the United States do when regional conflicts erupt?

There are several nonmilitary responses, which would be keeping with the principle of nonintervention, not "isolationism," which critics equate with being disengaged in world affairs. On the contrary, a sound foreign-military policy demands that the United States government uses its diplomatic corps to negotiate settlements between the warring—or near warring—nations. Rather than impose a settlement by force or threat of force, the United States should lead by example and resolve disputes, or, if a conflict is already underway, use its moral influence to halt the hostilities. The United States thus should refocus its military strategy in the new era to maintaining an adequate military force to protect the American people at home from aggression. The U.S. should withdraw its troops from overseas over the next couple of years and lead the community of nations to settle disputes diplomatically to avoid war around the world. Civil wars around the globe are indeed horrible. The United States can try to prevent them, but once started, it cannot end them militarily. The best we can hope for is justice to prevail, and for the factions to cease the hostilities and negotiate their differences.

The above guidelines are general. The specifics can be addressed once there is agreement in the country that the U.S. military must be used for the defense of the American people. U.S. national interests should be defined as maintenance of the territorial integrity of the republic and not the national boundaries of other countries. Entangling alliances have been the tripwire for war. They must be avoided.

The military budget can be reduced substantially. According to Cato Institute analyst Jeffrey V. Gerlach, writing in May 1992, *Pentagon Myths and Global Realities:The 1993 Military Budget*, U.S. military expenditures of $150 billion (in 1992 dollars) would be adequate to defend the country, allow the U.S. to be the world's dominant naval power, and make it possible to develop new technologies against any future threats. U.S. citizens should debate these proposals because they appear sound for safeguarding America's interests in the world today. Failure to reduce the military budget more than is currently proposed and not refocusing our military strategy could tempt future presidents to intervene around the globe. In addition, diminishing the military expenditures will have a positive effect on the economy—more products at lower prices and higher employment in areas where there currently are shortages—and thus produce a higher standard of living for the American people. Opponents of major reductions in military expenditures indeed have a weak case. Maintaining a larger military force in the 1990s than is necessary is not justifiable. It's now up to the American people to decide.

Social Security

If your neighbor who works in the investment field offered you a retirement program that was based on equal contributions from you and your employer with a promise that you will receive monthly benefits when you reach 65 years of age, you would probably want to know some specific details. What if your neighbor said the monthly benefits would be based on a formula on the amount that was contributed into your account. Today we don't know the exact amount you will receive but based on today's beneficiaries, you should receive "x" dollars per month. "How are my contributions invested?" you ask. "Well," says your neighbor, "our company borrows the excess money that isn't used to pay for the current retirees." You ask incredulously, "Isn't all my money invested in assets that will generate income and capital gains so my account accumulates a substantial nest egg?" "No," responds your neighbor, "My company borrows the excess money and pays interest on these IOUs so there will be a pool of money for future retirees." "But," you ask, "will there be enough money to pay benefits for future retirees?" Now, your neighbor is getting a little frustrated because you obviously do not understand the beauty of this plan. "Our future clients will be paying us premiums, most of which will be paid to you and other retirees so everyone will be a winner!" explains your neighbor. "I think I get it, but let me ask you this—how do you know you will have clients in the future? And, how do I know your company will be in business when I retire?" Your neighbor starts turning a little red and says, "Trust me."

If a private financial company offered this retirement plan to the public it would be prosecuted for fraud. By not segregating the clients' funds in a specific account but using the premiums to pay off past contributors, the company is conducting a Ponzi scheme (a fraudulent investment) or a chain letter. The initial "investors" benefit while those at the end of the chain lose all or most of their money. For a chain letter to work, more and more individuals must participate so that everyone can get paid off. Eventually, when a link or several links are broken, the chain collapses. The federal, state, or local government occasionally issues an alert about a chain letter being distributed, and warns the public not to participate. Yet, the most notorious chain letter of all time is being conducted by the federal government: Social Security.

The description of the neighbor's "retirement" plan is precisely how Social Security operates, but with a significant difference. Social Security is based on compulsory payroll taxes, while the neighbor's plan is voluntary, but still fraudulent. In short, fraud is fraud whether practiced by a private company or the government. Yet, Social Security has come to represent a secular shrine, an untouchable monument to America's mixed economy, a "compact" between society and the elderly. Like many mystical icons, the truth has been told repeatedly but presidents and members of Congress repeat the chant during every election year, "Don't mess with Social Security." How has one program that is clearly unethical and incorporating unsound economics, come to have such a revered status in a nation founded on both a strong moral base and free market principles?

The Social Security Act was passed in 1935, one of the centerpieces of FDR's New Deal program. Social Security was originally financed as a fully funded program, which meant the taxes collected would be saved, invested, and placed in a trust fund from which the accumulated returns would be used to pay future benefits. Support was gained for Social

Security because of fully funded financing. In short, the original Social Security program was no different than an actuarially sound private pension plan. In 1939, Congress amended the Social Security Act and began to replace the full-funding system with pay-as-you-go financing. Payments to individuals, which were to begin in 1942, were moved up and the first recipient of monthly Social Security benefits received her first check in January 1940. In the meantime, the trust fund had a substantial reserve by this time so Congress decided to reduce scheduled tax increases. "The 1939 amendments also added benefits for dependents of retired workers and initiated the survivors' insurance portion of the program with the addition of benefits for survivors of deceased workers."[4] Future amendments established disability insurance (1956), health insurance (1965) and indexed benefits (1972) so retirees' monthly checks would keep pace with inflation. By the late 1970s Social Security was in crisis and only a massive tax increase in 1977—the largest peacetime tax hike until then—kept the system going.

When Ronald Reagan took office in January 1981, Social Security was again facing a financial crisis. This time a bipartisan commission, appointed by the president and the congressional leadership, directed by Alan Greenspan, now chairman of the Federal Reserve Board, released its recommendations on 10 January 1983. The "solutions" to fix Social Security should not have been surprising; they included such major changes as higher taxes for both employees and employers, higher taxes for the self-employed, taxing some Social Security benefits for the first time, and bringing new federal workers and employees of nonprofit organizations under another system. Other provisions fine tuned the system, but the most important recommendation was the substantial tax hikes, which in 1992 reached 7.65 percent paid by both the employee and employer on $53,400 for Social Security. The maximum annual income of workers subject to the tax rise each year automatically.

Recent additional changes include raising the retirement age from 65 to 67 slowly starting in 2000. Over the past fifteen years, the "fixing" of Social Security is supposed to guarantee a substantial trust fund to pay the baby boom generation, which begins collecting benefits in 2012 (If the Social Security retirement age is untouched, they would begin to receive benefits in 2011.) By 2041, assuming nothing is done in terms of increasing taxes or reducing benefits in the future, the trust fund will be empty. However, if people live longer or the economy performs less than is forecast, the trust fund could be exhausted well before 2041.[5]

Analysts have described Social Security as the "system that works," and "one of America's biggest successes." Calling Social Security a "success" is like calling bank robbery an attractive career option because robbers who have not been apprehended undoubtedly have a relatively high standard of living. Social Security's proponents, nevertheless, fawn over the system's alleged accomplishments: income for the elderly, especially of the lowest-wage earners, surviving spouses and children, payments for disabled workers, and health insurance for retirees. Indeed, an impressive list of benefits. But, what about the cost? Social Security relies on compulsory taxation to provide benefits which can be—and are—provided in the private sector. To conclude that the "benefits" of a government program are worthwhile even though it is based on massive coercion, demonstrates the broken moral compass analysts operate with. Any time funds are compulsorily transferred from one individual to another, someone benefits at someone else's expense. This paradigm is untenable. It is based on the premise that the ends justify the means, a dangerous principle for society to uphold.

In a comprehensive collection of essays edited by Peter J. Ferrara, (*Social Security: Prospects for Real Reform*) several analysts, including Ferrara, make insightful critiques of the Social Security system from various perspectives—economic, social, and political. One of the most shocking conclusions is that for current workers the real rates for return on their contributions range from slightly negative to slightly positive, well below the stock market's return over the past sixty years, which included the crashes of 1929–33 and 1987! In short, Social Security is a poor alternative to investing in America's corporations, which create the jobs, manufacture the products, and provide the services that raise the standard of living in the country. A reasonable conclusion to draw from this: Social Security taxes cause the standard of living to be lower than it would otherwise be by reducing the amount of capital available for the private sector. In addition, Social Security lowers retirees' standard of living, by depriving them of the opportunity to invest their "contributions" in America's economic growth. Moreover, Social Security drives up the cost of labor, because hiring a worker makes the employer subject to Social Security taxes. But, the employer cannot pay higher costs and maintain the company's profit margins. Again, a reasonable conclusion about the impact of Social Security taxes is that it both lowers wages for working people and it reduces an employer's demand for labor, thereby leading to relatively high, permanent unemployment. Working people are therefore adversely affected in several ways; their wages are lowered, their ability to invest in established or emerging companies is hampered, and their future standard of living is reduced. And, of course, some workers—especially those at the bottom on the economic ladder—are not hired in the first place because they are "priced" out of the market. Social Security taxes have raised the cost of employing them, thus preventing them from even beginning to climb the economic ladder!

Social Security taxes clearly harm the economy and young workers—future recipients—who will have paid much more into the system than they will ever receive in benefits. Social Security also shortchanges the heirs of workers who die before they reach retirement age. Although spouses of deceased workers receive benefits, they receive less than they could have had available to them if the Social Security taxes (contributions) had been invested in an individual retirement account. An IRA is a sound vehicle for building an investment portfolio for retirement or an estate for one's heirs. Social Security taxes, however, preclude many people from establishing IRAs. People who earn $20–$40,000 per annum need their after-tax income for basic necessities and thus do not save because Social Security is viewed by them as their retirement package. A big mistake. A sound retirement program involves voluntary savings in common stocks, bonds, etc., not an intergenerational chain letter.

Furthermore, Social Security is neither a contract nor a compact. A contract is a voluntary agreement between the two parties who have to adhere to the conditions stipulated. Social Security is not a voluntary contract between the people and the federal government. It is based on compulsion and coercion. As the history of the past six decades has shown, Congress changes the rules and benefits when it wants to. The so-called social compact that the federal government entered into with the people is false. Congress has changed the law frequently, initially increasing benefits in the early years of the program and then cutting benefits of individuals and couples with adjusted gross income from other sources of more than $20,000 and $25,000, respectively. But, when catastrophic health insurance was passed several years ago, senior citizens protested vigorously even though they would receive these benefits by paying a premium from their monthly check. Congress repealed the catastrophic health provision. Were senior citizens expressing their disgust with another mandated program from the federal government? Or, did the seniors want the benefits but were unwilling to pay the costs? Senior citizens did not want these benefits even though they would have been subsidized. Three cheers for the seniors! Senior citizens revealed that change is possible when the Congress is inundated with protests. Will today's twenty-one to forty-six-year olds have the courage to protest social(istic) (in)security? Or, will they passively resign themselves to being taken to the cleaners by Uncle Sam . . . ? It's up to them.

Medicare

Medicare (health insurance) was established in 1965, one of the programs enacted by the federal government as part of Lyndon Johnson's Great Society. Medicare contains two parts, A and B. The former covers hospital bills and is funded by a tax on wages (1.45 percent for both employees and employers currently). The latter covers doctor's bills and other services financed primarily by premiums paid by the elderly, which is deducted from their monthly benefits, and partially by general taxes. Taxpayers, therefore, subsidize the elderly, who in some cases may have much higher incomes than the workers being taxed.

Currently, more than 34 million Americans are enrolled in Medicare. In 1993, Medicare expenditures totaled $130 billion, up from $64 million in 1966 (the first year of the program) and $32 billion in 1980. Medicare expenditures have clearly skyrocketed over the past two-and-a-half decades and are projected to reach $230 billion in 1998. In order to control Medicare's spiralling costs, legislation has been passed (1983 and 1992) to hold down reimbursement costs to hospitals and physicians, respectively. But, with the aging of the population, the most fundamental flaw of the program remains, relatively less taxpayers to pay for relatively more retirees in the decades ahead. In short, Medicare is another example of a chain letter; taxes are being paid by current workers for benefits received by present retirees. This program could self-destruct because expenditures will become much greater than outlays (assuming taxes are not raised), producing huge deficits which could mean either higher Medicare taxes and/or general taxes. Thus, future taxpayers will have to support the system or may revolt in anger over the crushing taxes needed to keep Medicare afloat. In other words, a major confrontation is developing, which is going to pit the elderly against their children and grandchildren.

A generational "war" appears to be the inevitable result of government meddling in the marketplace. As much as the proponents of both Social Security and Medicare do not want to admit it, social harmony is undermined by government programs that take from Peter and give to Paul. Instead of the elderly being treated with respect and dignity, they are becoming increasingly viewed by younger generations as society's burden, a view that makes euthanasia gain respectability as a way of dealing with senior citizens. But, there is a way out of course, which will be discussed in Chapter 7, so the elderly, especially poor retirees who are dependent for most of their living expenses on their monthly Social Security benefits, can enjoy their retirement without the fear of not having sufficient food, shelter, and medical care. The question is not can we do it, but do we have the courage to offer all the American people an opportunity to formulate a common sense program for retirement benefits. This is the one greatest challenge we face in the 1990s, and the time is ripe to phase-out Social Security and Medicare.

Medicaid

Medicaid was adopted in 1965 as yet another cornerstone of President Johnson's Great Society program. Initially, the program was intended to ensure that individuals would receive medical care even if they could not afford it. The federal government pays half the costs and the states the other half, with localities contributing in some states. The states administer Medicaid, set eligibility requirements, and offer a variety of services to recipients, under guidelines established by the federal government. Although Medicaid was supposed to be for poor or low-income families, "more and more of the program's resources are being devoted to the elderly, many of whom are essentially middle class . . ."[6]   *IN NURSING HOME*

Federal spending on Medicaid reached $85 billion in fiscal 1993, up from $52.5 billion a year earlier, and is projected to rise to $157 billion in 1998. Spending has grown 10 to 15 percent in most years since 1965. (In some years, spending increased 20–25 percent and jumped an astonishing 38 percent from 1991 to 1992.) And, with state governments paying for half the program, their budgets have been growing rapidly to pay for Medicaid as well as other social services, e.g., education, welfare, etc. The explosion in Medicaid expenditures should not come as a surprise to public officials or public policy analysts. When the government initiates an "entitlement" in society, demand will always outstrip supply; hence, rising costs.

The introduction of both Medicare and Medicaid in 1965 coincided with the acceleration of medical care price inflation in the United States. Although prices, in general, have increased more than four times in the past three decades, the "disinflation" of the past decade has not prevented health care costs from skyrocketing in recent years. So, with health care price inflation increasing faster than general price inflation in the economy, the usual scapegoats are blamed: doctors, insurance companies, drug companies, and litigating attorneys. Very few blame the catalyst, the government, which is now paying for nearly half of all medical costs. We are halfway to national health care!

There is probably no better example of how "good" intentions—providing health care for poor and low-income families—are not enough to develop a program that will achieve its objectives and be cost effective. Before we can tackle this issue, we must first agree on a fundamental principle, otherwise we will not be able to implement a sound solution to delivering medical care or any other service people want. There is no such thing as a positive entitlement. U.S. citizens—and noncitizens—do not have a right to food, clothing, shelter, education, medical care, welfare, etc. People have a right to pursue these objectives but no one is morally obligated to provide them to anyone. The government cannot provide these services unless it first appropriates resources from people; in other words, unless it engages in legal plunder. This is the challenge for the American people as we are about to enter the twenty-first century: how to assist the less fortunate among us without coercing the citizens of the country and plundering their incomes.

6

The Government's Money Monopoly

It is desirable that we use government to provide a stable monetary framework for a free economy...

--Milton Friedman

The abhorrence of the gold standard is inspired by the superstition that omnipotent governments can create wealth out of little scraps of paper.

--Ludwig von Mises

How would you like to be the most popular person in your neighborhood? Your town? Your county? Your state? How would you like to be the most popular person in the country, surpassing the adulation that even Madonna, Michael Jordan or Michael Jackson receives? How could you be so popular even if you cannot sing, dance, dunk a basketball, or make a career selling "sex"? Simple. Have an unlimited checking account. Impossible you say? No one has an "unlimited" checking account. Wrong! While the average American has to work 9 a.m. to 5 p.m. or risk his or her savings operating a business to obtain income so they can make deposits in their checking accounts, a government-created agency has the legal right to write a check for any amount.

What? Government officials not only have taxpayers' money at their disposal, but they also have the right to create an unlimited amount to boot. Isn't America a great country? And you thought only criminals could obtain money without working.

The government, specifically the Federal Reserve, can create money via its unlimited checking account. Is this good or bad for the economy? Is this *kosher*? Should the Federal Reserve have the power to create money "out of thin air"? Before exploring the government's money monopoly, we need to discuss the origin of money and banking. We shall see that government did not originate money, but that a general medium of exchange can only occur when people voluntarily agree to use a valuable commodity. We shall also lay to rest in this chapter the myth, first promulgated by Karl Marx and then uncritically accepted by non-Marxists, that the free market is subject to violent swings in output and employment and therefore a wise, all-knowing, all-powerful government must step in to "smooth out" the business cycle. For the past several decades, public officials have embraced this assertion—the inherent instability of the free market—to rationalize monetary socialism. Bankers also wanted a banking cartel at the turn of the century so they could benefit from a central bank's money-creating powers. The culmination of this process, the agitation for a centralized monetary institution, was the passage of the Federal Reserve Act in December 1913. The events leading to the adoption of monetary socialism in the United States is just as fascinating as the enactment of the income tax earlier that same year. Together, these two institutions cemented substantial government control over the economy.

Money

The castaways on Gilligan's Island, a popular television show in the 1960s, did not need money. Stranded on an uncharted island, the Skipper, Gilligan, and their companions required that the most basic human needs be satisfied in order to survive. There was no local economy in which they could trade for food, clothing, etc., so the castaways had to be self-sufficient. It was them against nature. They had no need for "money." Even if they had money (dollar bills) it would have been useless because there were no products to purchase.

On Gilligan's Island, the castaways realized they must engage in productive activity if they were to survive. A fish net is made, berries are picked, a field is cleared, trees and plants are cut for housing, and logs are gathered for firewood. The castaways have thus established an economy, engaging in direct exchange, barter, in order to satisfy their needs. In other words, the goods they have "created" are consumed and exchanged for other goods they need. They are able to produce and consume without "money."

Let's now assume the Skipper and Gilligan built a small boat and they sailed to a neighboring island where they met some natives who were anxious to trade with them. The problem that arose was that the Skipper and Gilligan did not have any goods the natives wanted except a necklace made of relatively rare shells Gilligan was wearing. He found the shells on the beach and he made a necklace. Lo and behold, the castaways were now able to trade the shells found on their island for foodstuffs and other items the natives have in relative abundance. Shells become a general medium of exchange; a money economy is born. Not only were the shells used for decorative purposes, as jewelry and other types of ornaments, but now all the market participants realized that they could be exchanged for other goods. The natives also used the shells, let's assume, for their curative powers. The castaways on Gilligan's Island began to trade the shells with each other for the items they produced. A local money economy on Gilligan's Island now existed, as well as an "international" money economy with the neighboring island.

The important lesson from the above is that "money" can only arise from the exchange process. Money was not invented, it evolved. On the island economy, the people began to trade the goods they produced for a valuable commodity— shells. In turn, they traded the shells for goods they need and wanted, hence, the division of labor and specialization could blossom in this relatively primitive economy.

No "government" decreed that something, let alone "paper," was money and therefore buyers and sellers were free to use whatever commodity they wanted as the medium of exchange. What if Gilligan or the Skipper had handed the native some U.S. dollar bills in exchange for food? The natives would have asked (assuming they could communicate effectively), what do we do with these bits of paper. The Skipper may have replied that this is money where we come from. The natives may have countered: "Money? What can you do with this paper except burn it, and we have plenty of things to use as kindling. Why are you trying to obtain goods from us for things that have no value for us?" The Skipper and Gilligan probably looked at each other in disbelief. These natives don't seem to understand that dollar bills can buy a lot of valuable things in the United States. Ah, therein lies the mystery.

Why do Americans accept paper dollars so readily when Gilligan's native friends were unwilling to trade their products for them? We have learned an important lesson: paper cannot function as money unless . . . . What if the Skipper and Gilligan handed the natives a ten dollar bill and told them they could exchange this paper note for shells (weighing 1 gram), a good the natives valued very highly?

The skeptical natives were suspicious and agreed, but were uneasy about giving up valuable goods for the promise of receiving valuable shells in the future. They were initially reluctant to accept this "money substitute" for the "real thing." The natives exchanged goods for a ten dollar bill, and the Skipper and Gilligan realized they had to go back to their island and return with a one gram shell, otherwise the outlook for trading with their neighbors would be greatly diminished. The natives would lose faith with Gilligan and the Skipper. Moreover, they would have cheated the natives, obtaining a valuable commodity for, in the eyes of the natives, a worthless piece of paper. Gilligan and the Skipper rushed back to the island, took one shell from their meager stockpile and returned to the natives to redeem their ten dollar bill for one shell. The natives were impressed. They thought Gilligan and the Skipper had pulled a fast one. The natives told them they would be happy to trade their goods for dollar bills as long as redeemability was prompt. Gilligan and the Skipper were ecstatic. Rather than load up the boat with shells all the time they could just bring dollar bills, get goods in exchange and redeem the paper money soon thereafter. A redeemable paper money economy was established.

The Gilligan economy has evolved from barter (direct exchange) to money (commodities, indirect exchange) to "paper money" (paper redeemable for real money). The castaways and their neighbors were producing, consuming, and surviving. What limited their standard of living was technology and capital goods, not a scarcity of money. The Professor on Gilligan's Island had knowledge about building things, but the lack of equipment to construct any elaborate machinery prevented the castaways from markedly increasing their standard of living. Nevertheless, some tools could be made, which would allow the castaways to increase their food production, make additional clothing, etc. Although not thriving, the inhabitants of Gilligan's Island were surviving much better than they had expected because they began to trade with people on a neighboring island and nobody on Gilligan's Island became unemployed! The wonders of free trade!

Let's now introduce an institution in the economy that would provide a useful service and help facilitate trade between the two islands.

Banking

The Howells, a wealthy castaway couple, decided to open a bank with their own dollars and the shells they had accumulated. As a banker in the United States, Mr. Howell had experience in financial services. He and his wife opened the Howell Bank, accepting shells for safekeeping, which were redeemable in "dollars" they brought ashore, let's say $11,000 in various denominations. For this service, the other castaways paid the bank a small fee. In addition, the bank offered another service. For another small fee, depositors could open an account with their shells and write a "check" to sellers of goods stating that the bank would redeem this order for real money—shells. Demand deposits were thus created.

With dollar bills and checks redeemable from the Howell Bank in shells, the bank is providing valuable service and earning income. The bank, moreover, operated on a 100 percent reserve basis. That is, the bank had on deposit sufficient shells to meet any withdrawals at any time for all the paper money and demand deposits outstanding. In short, there could never be a run on the bank which "ruptured" it. The bank was bankrupt-proof.

Mr. Howell was operating a deposit bank with 100 percent reserves, earning fees and facilitating trade because the castaways did not have to carry shells with them. Mr. Howell was not content, however, with earning only fees, and besides, his companions were not redeeming their dollars and demand deposits for shells. Even the natives began using the bank, having sailed to Gilligan's Island after realizing the castaways were hard working, honest people. Mr. Howell decided to make a loan to Gilligan who wanted to hire some natives to clear a field and start a new farm. Instead of lending Gilligan some of his own shells (ten grams let's assume) to earn interest on the loan, Mr. Howell loaned him one hundred dollars from his supply of dollars, or he could have loaned him some of the shells already on deposit. If Mr. Howell's bank had, for example, eighty one-gram shells on deposit and $500 in dollar bills and $300 in demand deposits outstanding (in "circulation"), the bank was solvent. Mr. Howell had "created," in effect, a claim for another 10 shells by lending Gilligan $100 in bills, or he may have opened a checking account for him with this amount. Either way, Mr. Howell inflated the supply of money in the economy. He made it possible for Gilligan to inject more money into the economy to buy goods and/or purchase services. Moreover, the Howell Bank was now at great risk, because there were more dollar bills and demand deposits outstanding than shells on reserve, eighty shells in reserve, ninety claims to shells ($500, $300 demand deposits, $100 in new bills or deposits). In short, the bank was subject to a bank run if depositors become suspicious that Mr. Howell was engaging in fractional reserve banking; that is, creating receipts of shells that did not exist. To people in the economy, the new receipts—bills or checks— looked like any of the previous ones, so people were not particularly worried, at least initially.

From a legal point of view, Mr. Howell's increase in the bank's liabilities—claims to real money—without an offsetting increase in real money was fraudulent. The Howell Bank could not possibly redeem all its liabilities in real money at any time, the hallmark of a sound deposit or warehouse bank. What are the economic effects of the Howell's inflationary policy?

Money, Banking, and Inflation

Before "banking" was established on Gilligan's Island, the castaways traded among themselves and eventually traded with the neighboring island natives. The prices of goods and services on the island and between the islands were established by the law of supply and demand. For example, a dozen fish may have exchanged for a bushel of berries; one-half bushel of berries may have purchased a dozen eggs. These exchange ratios were the economy's prices. When shells were also traded for these goods, anyone could determine the price of commodities for shells, the economy's money. If one shell could be exchanged for one dozen fish, a bushel of berries and two dozen eggs, then the array of prices, the voluntary payments between buyers and sellers, were established. These prices were not fixed forever but represented the economic relationship between money and goods at a particular point in time. If the supply of fish increased, for example, the exchange ratio would change to two dozen fish for one shell. If the berry crop increased, a new exchange ratio would be, say, one-and-a-half bushels for one shell, and if the chickens began laying eggs faster, three dozen eggs would now exchange for one shell. Conversely, if the supply of goods decreased, a shell would not buy as much. So, if the fish supply diminished, a shell would only buy one-half dozen fish; if the berry crop was infested by bugs, a shell would only be able to buy a half bushel of berries. And if the chickens' output of eggs declined, one shell would only buy one dozen eggs.

Prices on the island's economy would thus fluctuate according to the amount of goods available—the supply side. What about the demand side? If there was an increase in demand for berries, the price of a bushel of berries would rise to one-and-one-half shells. But if the demand for berries rises, the demand for other goods—fish and eggs—would probably fall, as would their prices, reflecting a shift in demand for goods in the economy. But if the prices of all goods rose, with one bushel of berries increasing to two shells (instead of one), one dozen fish now two shells (instead of one), and two dozen eggs exchanging for two shells (instead of one), then buyers must have more money to offer in the marketplace for these goods. Where did they get the money? If people obtained the money—shells—by combing the beaches and digging them out, they have added to the supply of shells and prices will adjust according to the new supply-demand relationships in the marketplace. The new real money was obtained by using resources—labor and tools—to transform the naturally found shells into a useful commodity in the marketplace. As we saw earlier, people chose shells to use an money, it was not imposed on them by "government." However, what if someone borrowed money from the Howell Bank, which issued new receipts for nonexistent shells, what are the consequences?

As we saw above, the creation of so-called pseudo receipts is inflation—monetary inflation. Thus, introducing pseudo receipts into the marketplace to purchase goods is to engage in fraud. In the marketplace:

> Production leads to "purchase" of money, which leads to "sale" of money for goods.[1]

This is the essence of a market economy; the output of producers is used to purchase money which, in turn, is used to purchase goods desired by all producers—workers and business owners. In other words, the money is essentially a "claim" on goods produced in the economy. But, to have a claim on goods, an individual must have produced something prior in order to exercise his claim with real money. Using pseudo-receipts is tantamount to theft, claiming goods without first being a producer, which is exactly what a robber or thief does! A robber or thief claims goods—"your money or your life"—without having produced in the economy. Monetary inflation therefore is a subtle form of theft.

What about the economic consequences? Monetary inflation, creating claims to real money which cannot be met, causes prices to rise. If the Howell Bank simply increased the supply of bills or deposits, the first recipients of the new money could now purchase the existing supply of goods, out-bidding other consumers. Moreover, the purchasing power of the monetary unit would fall, because the supply of money—the demand side—was increasing and people would bid up the prices of the available supply of goods. As the new money spreads through the economy, people who have received the new money last or not at all, would have to pay higher prices. Even if their incomes increased belatedly, the prices they paid for goods would have increased first. They were the losers during the "inflationary" spiral. The people whose incomes had increased faster than the prices they paid for goods were clearly the winners in the inflationary spiral. Thus, to prevent "winners" and "losers" in an economy, monetary inflation—the injection of pseudo-receipts into the economy—must never begin.

On Gilligan's Island, the creation of pseudo-shell-receipts, whether an outright issuance of more paper money, or making loans from depositors' funds or crediting an individual's checking account, raised the prices of goods and services over time. Price inflation is thus a distortion of the economy. In a sound economy, prices fall because the output of goods increases while the supply of money is relatively stable. On the island, if a better net were made, or the Professor discovered a way to increase the yield of the berry trees, goods, which became relatively more abundant than money, fall in price, thereby increasing the standard of living for everyone. Deflation, a slowly falling drop in prices, is a bonanza for the economy—more goods, greater consumption at lower prices, more money available for retirement, thus a higher standard of living in the future, also.

Inflation redistributes wealth to the initial receivers of new money from individuals who pay higher prices for goods and are "last on line" to receive the new money. In short, inflation is a form of taxation, "taxing" the incomes of the buyers who have to pay higher prices. This tax falls most heavily on low- and middle-income individuals and retirees.

On Gilligan's Island, assume there are several dozen castaways instead of the original seven in the 1960s television series. If there are elderly, families with small children, and other households, the injection of pseudo-receipts into the economy would raise the price of food and other necessities, thus lowering the standard of living of the elderly who may be eking out an existence doing some small-scale farming or caring for the young children. The elderly did not earn much income because their output is low. In addition, they were unlikely recipients of new money from the bank. When the new money was injected into the economy, the most likely recipients were the banker himself, his close friends, and others who were willing to borrow from the bank. These individuals were the clear winners during the inflationary cycle, gaining at the expense of the elderly and others in the economy.

We have observed how "inflation" is initiated and unfolds in a simple economy. The monetary principles are universal truths. "Printing" money causes what is generally called inflation. A sustained increase in virtually all prices can only occur if either the supply of goods drops continuously, or the supply of money rises steadily. Inasmuch as the supply of goods has been increasing for centuries and even over the past few decades, price rises can only be caused by a steady rise in the supply of money. Does this mean that the economy's chosen commodity should not be increased? On the contrary, the economy's monetary unit, the one gram shell on Gilligan's Island, or the gold, silver, tobacco, salt, etc., used throughout western civilization has non-monetary uses. A greater supply of the commodity is always beneficial to the economy. But as a monetary unit, an increase in the supply of money, only raises prices, i.e., lowers the purchasing power of the monetary unit. Thus, there is no general economic benefit to an increase in the supply of money.

"We come to the startling truth that it *doesn't* matter what the supply of money is. Any supply will do as well as any other supply. The free market will simply adjust by changing the purchasing power, or effectiveness of the . . . unit."[2]

Despite the elementary truth about money, prices and the economy, the proposition that monetary inflation is both necessary and desirable for economic growth is one of the great fallacies in economic thought. As we have seen, inflating the supply of money (1) raises prices unevenly, benefitting some people at the expense of other people, (2) prevents prices from reaching their "natural" lower level, and (3) imposes a "tax" on people who hold money as prices rise. In short, monetary inflation is an economic and social disaster, but most economists, as well as virtually all public officials, support inflationary policies, euphemistically called "easy" money. As we will see below, so-called easy money policies also generate the cycle of boom and bust. Despite all the negative consequences of inflating the supply of money, easy money is considered one of the great elixirs for the economy. Nothing could be further from the truth. Throughout American history, government intervention in money and banking has caused havoc in the economy. Instead of freeing money and banking from government domination, the federal government in effect "socialized" our monetary system in 1913. The American people have been paying the price ever since in terms of economic instability.

From Real Money to Paper Money

Businesses have to earn their profits by satisfying consumer needs. No one's profits are guaranteed. With profits ephemeral, businesses have to constantly strive to satisfy consumers in order to reap profits in the free-market. But profits can be (somewhat) guaranteed if potential competitors are prevented from entering the marketplace or if prices can be artificially maintained above their free market level. Voluntary cartels in various industries can try to achieve these objectives by lowering supply and maintaining higher than equilibrium prices, but without the force of law how can new companies be prevented from entering the marketplace and how can prices be kept above their free-market level? The key, therefore, for big business is to embrace government intervention to achieve their objectives while paying lip service to *laissez faire* and free enterprise.

As Gabriel Kolko states in *The Triumph of Conservatism:*

> Despite the large number of mergers, and the growth in the absolute size of many corporations, the dominant tendency in the American economy toward the beginning of this century was toward growing competition. Competition was unacceptable to many big businesses and financial interests, and the merger movement was to a large extent a reflection of voluntary, unsuccessful business efforts to bring irresistible competitive trends under control. Although profit was always a consideration, rationalization of the market was frequently a necessary prerequisite for maintaining long-term profits. As new competitors sprang up, and as economic power was diffused throughout an expanding nation, it became apparent to many important businessmen that only the national government could rationalize the economy.[3]

Kolko, unsympathetic to *laissez faire*, nevertheless targets as the causal factor for massive regulation of the economy, the desire by key business leaders to have the federal government intervene on their behalf in the name of "efficiency," "stability," and "progress."

As the country grew, more banks sprang up to meet the needs of business. Wall Street banks therefore had more competition. According to Kolko's thesis, financial interests saw their rivals as threats who had to be brought into line. The stage was set to do for banking what the federal government had been doing for other sectors of the economy.

Meanwhile, the Gold Standard Act of 1900 "placed the United States officially on a monometallic gold standard. All paper was to be redeemable in gold, and silver continued as a subsidiary metal."[4] The discovery of gold in South Africa and Alaska in the 1890s increased the world's supply of the yellow metal and raised prices in the United States by nearly 50 percent from 1897 to 1914. But, with fractional reserve banking still functioning, the total supply of money increased dramatically during this period.

The Panic of 1907 highlighted what hard-money and sound banking proponents had been criticizing for decades, that fractional reserves inflate the money supply and generate unstable economic conditions and destabilize the banking system. The banking establishment and both political parties, however, concluded that central banking was the answer to economic stability. So the die was cast to centralize monetary and banking decisions in the name of reform. The full story is available elsewhere, but the events leading to the passage of the Federal Reserve Act in 1913 completed a watershed year in American history, the triumph of statism—quasi-socialism.

The plan for a U.S. central bank was discussed by several prominent bankers, including Paul Warburg of the investment banking firm, Kuhn, Loeb & Co.; Henry Davision of the House of Morgan; Charles Norton of the Trust National Bank; Frank A. Vanderlip of National City Bank; and Senator Nelson W. Aldrich, Republican of Rhode Island "who had headed the pro-central banking studies of the Congressionally created National Monetary Commission."[5] The powerful financial interests represented at this secret meeting on Jekyll Island off the Georgia coast in December 1910 hammered out what essentially became the Federal Reserve Act signed by President Wilson in December 1913. Whether this was a deep dark "conspiracy" can be argued endlessly. The creation of the Federal Reserve was another example of individuals laying their plans out for federal legislation to achieve their objective. All cooperative actions are "conspiracies" if we define conspiracy as two or more individuals formulating a plan to carry out their objectives. By this broad definition marriage is a "conspiracy." But, in the final analysis the Federal Reserve Act socialized the monetary system.

The "theory" and practice of the Federal Reserve was to prevent panics and bank runs forever because of the power and prestige of the central bank. However, the Fed's inflationary policy during the 1920s stimulated the economy triggering the stock market and real estate booms. This artificial stimulation culminated in the crash of 1929 and the subsequent downturn, during which the speculative investments made during the previous decade were liquidated. President Hoover, the first New Dealer, and then President Roosevelt intervened massively in the economy. Hoover hiked tariffs to unprecedented levels in 1930, touching off a worldwide wave of protectionism and deepening the depression. The second phase of America's shift to a quasi-socialized economy was underway. A criticism of the Hoover-Roosevelt New Deal policies are beyond the scope of this discussion, but the general view that Hoover was a *laissez-faire* president is contradicted not only by the historical record but with his own words during the 1932 presidential campaign.

> We might have done nothing. That would have been utter ruin. Instead, we met the situation with proposals to private business and to Congress of the most gigantic program of economic defense and counter attack ever evolved in the history of the Republic. We put it into action.[6]

In short, Hoover was an activist, interventionist president and did not sit on his hands as the economy spiralled downward into oblivion. The federal government's policies exacerbated the depression and left an indelible mark on the American people's collective psyche—the federal government should be responsible for the people's economic security.

The price for this economic security is the $4 trillion-plus debt the federal government has accumulated, virtually all of it since 1913 when it was a measly $1.9 billion.

The Boom-Bust Cycle

The Federal Reserve was supposed to coordinate inflating the supply of money and credit and banish forever the cycle of boom and bust, that is, stabilize the economy. It has not happened—and will not happen. The reason the Federal Reserve has not been able to "stabilize" the economy is not because of venal businessmen, greedy workers, bad harvests, oil price shocks, or natural disasters. The reason is the Fed has continued to inflate the supply of credit through the fractional reserve banking system. Every panic, depression, or recession, that has occurred in American history has always been preceded by a period of "easy" money. Yet, most economists support the current monetary and banking system as the ideal arrangement. What they argue for is better management of a socialized sector of the economy, as if better "management" of the Soviet Union's collectivist economy would have generated prosperity!

We have discussed the relationship between money and prices and now it is time to expand the analysis to show how credit conditions are related to economic fluctuations. The conventional view of economists is that the Federal Reserve is the guardian of the dollar's integrity and that a "little" stimulus—easy money—is necessary for economic growth. Well, increasing the money supply, as we have seen, lowers its purchasing power and easy money (or loose credit) generates the boom-bust cycle.

A boom is generated when new money in the banking system is available to be loaned to business. The new money is initially created when the Federal Reserve purchases assets, usually U.S. government securities, by writing a check on itself, thus literally creating money out of thin air. Sellers of these securities are brokerage firms, investment banks, life insurance companies, etc. These checks, in turn, are deposited in commercial banks, thereby increasing the banking system's reserves. The banks' acquisition of these funds make it possible for businessmen throughout the country to obtain loans at lower interest rates initially because the supply of loanable funds has increased relative to the demand for them. But the bank loans do not represent genuine savings of the public. Instead, the banks are lending inflationary credit, i.e., money that has been created out of thin air.

The primary beneficiaries of the central bank's credit inflation are the capital-goods industries. The decline in interest rates that accompanies credit expansion is a signal to businessmen that the public prefers to save and invest more than before. Many entrepreneurs thus will borrow from the banks and invest in more raw materials, machinery, and plant equipment. Subsequently, there will be an expansion both in employment and output in the capital-goods industries, e.g., steel, construction, cement, aluminum, machine tools, etc. The boom begins.

The capital-goods industries, however, depend upon a sustained increase in savings to justify their expansion. Unfortunately, the public's voluntary savings—via purchases of common stocks, long-term bonds, and other financial instruments—are not great enough to permit businessmen to continue the increased production in these industries. If the Federal Reserve, however, injects more credit into the banking system, the boom can last awhile longer because new bank loans to the capital-goods industries will allow them to maintain their higher rate of production. But, when price inflation heats up and interest rates begin to skyrocket because the new money has caused prices to rise and lenders to demand a purchasing power premium, the Fed predictably "tightens" monetary conditions to prevent inflation from accelerating.

However, price inflation does not have to occur during a boom. The "stability" of prices in the 1920s fooled most analysts into believing that the Fed had achieved its objective, sustained prosperity without inflation. But, in a growing economy with a sound monetary system, prices gradually fall as output expands. The Fed, in effect, prevented this "natural" phenomenon from occurring in the 1920s and generated monetary conditions which made a correction inevitable. The severity and extent of the depression reflects the government's interventionism as opposed to its alleged hands-off policy.

When the credit inflation ends, a portion of the boom's production is revealed to have been malinvested. These malinvestments are liquidated during the adjustment process, i.e., a depression. During a depression, labor (laid-off workers) and equipment (from bankrupt companies) must be reallocated to production processes that more accurately reflect the public's true consumption and investment preferences.

As Ludwig von Mises describes in *Human Action: A Treatise on Economics:*

> The wavelike movement affecting the economic system, the recurrence of periods of depression, is the unavoidable outcome of the attempts, repeated again and again, to lower the gross market rate of interest by means of credit expansion. There is no means of avoiding the final collapse of a boom brought about by credit expansion. The alternative is only whether the crisis should come sooner as the result of a voluntary abandonment of further credit expansion or later as a final and total catastrophe of the currency involved.[7]

And as Elgin Groseclose explains, cheap money has other consequences.

> Despite the tragic history of depreciating currencies advocates of monetary expansion continue to be lured by the prospect of cheap money—easier credit, abundant purchasing

power for everyone. Paradoxically, the effects are the opposite, and here we find the core of the moral malaise implicit in the process—that avarice, the desire for unearned wealth, is self-defeating.[8]

The lesson is therefore clear: to avoid creating a "steroid" economy—artificially pumping up the manufacturing sector and consumer spending—the Federal Reserve must not create money out of thin air! The Fed, however, is creating money because the federal government has been on a spending spree since the Great Depression. For, what the federal government doesn't raise in taxes, compliments of the Sixteenth Amendment, the Federal Reserve can either purchase the government's debt directly or purchase existing debt so banks and other financial institutions can purchase the flood of new government securities to cover Washington's annual deficits.

The policies of tax, spend, borrow and inflate are threatening the economy's health. We are at a crossroads just like the American people who faced the Depression of 1893 and the Panic of 1907. Back then, the economic and political elites opted for statism in 1913, an income tax, and monetary socialism. We desperately need a change in the 1990s to insure sustainable prosperity in the twenty-first century. If we choose wisely, a tax free America will be a reality. Otherwise, we will see government grow, the productive sector shrink, and unemployment increase. America has come too far to allow quasi-socialism to be our legacy for future generations.

7

Transforming the Public Sector:

The Birth of a Tax-Free America

The wealth of society is in proportion to the productive efforts of the individuals who compose that society, and government has nothing to do with it—beyond the negative function of maintaining order and protecting property. *People make wealth; government can only take it.*

--Frank Chodorov

Our mixed economy was supposed to deliver the American people to the Promised Land—the elimination of poverty, better housing and health care for all citizens, a well-educated population, a moderating of the business cycle, increasing employment opportunities, and an end to social-racial strife. Since President Johnson declared a "war" on poverty in the mid-1960s, the federal government has spent trillions of dollars on dozens of programs which were supposed to lift people up the economic ladder. With less than a stellar track record in alleviating poverty, government is called upon to spend more money because not enough money, according to proponents of welfare statism, has been spent! But, in the *Wall Street Journal* 19 December 1991 Peter Drucker wrote, ". . . government has proved incompetent at solving social problems. Virtually every success we have scored has been achieved by nonprofits." Drucker, one of the country's leading management experts, has written several books and hundreds of articles about sound management procedures as well as tackling the big issues, the U.S. economy's problems. As one of the first advocates of "privatization," he now proposes an adjunct policy, "nonprofitization," as a way modern societies gracefully eliminate their mismanaged welfare bureaucracies. As Drucker points out, there is no lack of talent or resources to solve America's social ills. "What is needed," however, "is a public policy that establishes the nonprofits as the country's first line of attack on its social problems."

In addition to the nonprofits, the private-profit sector can be recruited to assist in the development of programs that will improve the quality of life of the American people. Currently, the old way of thinking . . . "there is a problem therefore we need a government program" has proven ineffective and costly. To continue the tax, borrow, and spend policies of the past would be no different than if the former Soviet Union had continued to rely on central planning and its bureaucracy to deliver goods and services to its people. The Soviet Union not only doesn't exist anymore, but privatization there is proceeding, albeit ever so slowly. Because the old ways didn't work and could not be made to work, the Soviets could not square the circle. An economy cannot be successful without private property, a free price system, and a sound money and banking system. The Russians still lack these social institutions and that is why their economy is mired in depression. We, therefore, should learn from their experiment in total socialism: any degree of socialism causes economic distortions and social instability. The sooner the American people realize this fundamental truth, the sooner we will be on the road to sustainable prosperity.

This chapter will outline a framework for a tax-free America. The proposals presented here will cause little if any (financial) pain to the American people. As with any restructuring of society, there will be some individuals who may initially be worse off economically than before, but this will be a fleeting phenomenon. The blueprint's foundation—a free market—should make it clear that the economy will flourish because the heavy hand of the state will be lifted from the American people's work, production, and trading. In short, the proposals will liberate the American people from Washington just as the colonists were liberated from the British Empire more than two hundred years ago.

The American people's chains must be broken once and for all peacefully. The United States government has created an empire at home (and some would say overseas, too) which means less freedom and prosperity for the American people. Five thousand years of taxation throughout the world has shown that the people pay and pay and the ruling elites prosper. We can end the ruling elite's stranglehold on the American people. In other societies, the people will have to break their own chains, but they can learn from us again; just as America established the rights of man in the Declaration of Independence in the seventeenth century, we need a revival of those principles as we enter the twenty-first century. As Thomas Jefferson wrote: "a little rebellion, now and then, is a good thing."[1]

A rebellion is brewing in the land, but public officials are oblivious to the discontent, believing—clinging—to the notion a slight mid-course correction is all the economy needs to keep the people happy and subservient. Public officials and their academic apologists are trying to square the circle, trying to make the welfare state viable. The American people, in general, know there is something fundamentally wrong with the country, but more Americans need to be introduced or reintroduced to their philosophical heritage. The "shock" treatment prescription—*Tax-Free 2000*—is both necessary and possible. All we need is not to let the ruling elite con us, again.

The Blueprint

Social Security, Medicare, and Medicaid

The federal government has become an unmanageable organization. Like a leviathan swallowing up small fish, the federal government will suck up (the people's money resources) to the tune of $1.34 trillion in fiscal 1995, which begins on October 1, 1994, and will spend a substantial amount of money ($1.52 trillion) to allegedly improve the American people's lives. For all these and previous expenditures, we have not arrived in the Promised Land; and until the government is completely restructured, America's economic performance will continue to be erratic at best! Sound economic analysis, not ideology, dictates that the goals pursued by public officials cannot be accomplished by government spending. In short, our experiment in the mixed economy must be acknowledged a failure. This failure, however, is due to ideology; the belief that government is society's preeminent problem solver, that redistributing wealth (legal plunder) is an appropriate means to assist people and fund programs, and that "easy" money is a necessary "lubricant" for the economy.

Government succeeds when it adheres to its proper, minimal role in society. When government goes beyond its role as peacekeeper, it can only achieve other goals by engaging in legal plunder and distorting the economy's productive structure. These distortions tend to be cumulative. Economic crises are therefore virtually inevitable once government spending, taxation, borrowing, and inflating reach the point of hampering production and causing permanent unemployment. The cumulative distortions in the United States are reaching dangerously close to the point of a full-fledged economic crisis. A crisis, however, can be averted.

Government—at all levels—tries to do too much. To change the structure of the federal government, Social Security, Medicare, Medicaid, and interest on the national debt must be phased out.

To make the federal government manageable and achieve the goal of *Tax-Free 2000*, the following reforms will be discussed: obtaining revenue to pay for the nation's defense, phasing out Social Security so that virtually all beneficiaries do not receive less than they currently receive, providing medical coverage for retirees and the poor, and addressing the national debt burden.   These expenditures have been growing rapidly in recent years, except for defense spending which has actually been declining. They have been considered "untouchable" and politically off-limits. No more. They must be phased out.

Although a general blueprint will be presented below, it would be presumptuous to think that a detailed version of what a tax-free America would look like is possible. While some issues may not be completely resolved here, the guiding principle, keep the government confined to its legitimate role, will assure that the people's resources will be used by them according to their values. The ruling elite therefore will have to obtain money the old-fashioned way, they'll have to earn it.

All major federal taxes will be eliminated on 1 January 1997. (This is not to endorse the continuation of legal plunder. Taxation should end immediately. If, after reading *Tax-Free 2000,* the American people want to end taxation sooner, so be it!) The personal income tax, corporate income tax, Social Security, payroll tax, and excise taxes will be ended on New Year's Day 1997. The gasoline "tax," however, is in reality a user fee and will remain as long as the federal government controls the interstate highway system. But, during the transition to a tax-free America, the highway system could be sold to either private investors or the states. Preferably, private investors should purchase the highways rather than the states, because the less government involvement in resource alloca- tion, the healthier the economy will be.

In fiscal 1995, individual federal income taxes will reach $597.2 billion, payroll taxes $492.1 billion and corpo- rate payments $141.1 billion to Uncle Sam. If revenue is reduced by $1,230.4 billion, expenditures must be reduced accordingly or the budget deficit would increase by nearly $1.23 trillion. What expenditures will be cut? First, we begin with the $500 billion expenditures mentioned above. More specifically, agriculture, education, natural resources, research and development, foreign aid, transportation, energy, space, grants to states and cities, environmental protection, etc., all the cherished programs the American people have been told (propagandized) improve the quality of life in the country. In short, we have been conditioned to believe that the country would go to hell in a handbasket if these programs did not exist. This is rather peculiar since each program benefits, at most, only several million people out of a population of 260 million.

To assert, therefore, that the "people's" well-being would be adversely affected by the elimination of what, at best, can be described as a massive transfer of wealth is disingenuous. The recipients of the government's largesse, as well as the programs' employees, would be the only ones who would initially suffer when these programs are eliminated. But, with nearly $1.23 trillion in federal taxes not being collected, there would be an enormous initial and continuing stimulus to the economy. The deadweight of tax collection and processing, as well as the bureaucracies that regulate and thus hamper productive activities, would be eliminated. With the elimination of this deadweight spending the people's expenditures will reflect their demand for goods and services, including their annual philanthropic contributions, which totaled $125 billion in 1992. How much would charitable contributions increase? No one knows for sure, but it would be substantial because public opinion polls list charitable contributions as the number one expenditure people would make if they received a financial windfall. And, $1.23 trillion is a windfall in anyone's calculations!

In one stroke, a substantial portion of the federal budget's expenditures has been eliminated. Of the remaining budget, Social Security, Medicare, and Medicaid, will be phased out as soon as possible. One key to a Social Security phase-out is that beneficiaries continue to file a 1040 form every year based on the current tax law. Ending the income tax means Social Security recipients have greater after-tax income because they would no longer be paying taxes on dividends, interest, capital gains, pensions, and annuities. Their tax savings, therefore, must be deducted from their Social Security monthly checks, otherwise they would be getting a huge windfall. Their Social Security payments are made possible by taxing current workers. Social Security beneficiaries, therefore, would receive the same after-tax income in a tax-free America.

If a retired couple has a $30,000 income, $12,000 in Social Security payments, a $12,000 taxable pension, and $6,000 in taxable interest, their tax liability would be approximately $900. The elimination of the federal income tax should reduce their annual Social Security payment by that amount, because the couple is, in effect, paying their own Social Security with the $900 federal taxes, but there is more. If this couple lives in a private house, they pay property taxes, which, as we saw in Chapter 3, primarily pays for education. If this couple pays $4,000 in property taxes, $2,500 of which pays for public schools, they would be exempt from this levy because the public schools will be on a user fee basis or privatized. Thus, another $2,500 would be deducted from Social Security benefits for a total of $3,900, leaving the couple with approximately the same annual income.

A retired couple earning $50,000, which includes an additional $10,000 of taxable interest and $10,000 in wages, would pay $4,800 in federal income taxes and $1,540 in Social Security taxes (the worker is assumed to bear both the employer and employee share of the payroll tax). The total tax liability in this case is approximately $6,330, which, of course, would not be paid in 1997, thereby reducing the couple's benefits by this amount. If their property taxes are higher because they live in a more affluent area, let's say $5,000, and $3,600 is the educational component, the couple's Social Security benefits would be reduced by the amount of property taxes they no longer would be paying. Outlays for Social Security would drop dramatically, and should be completely eliminated no later than 2010. To fund the remaining Social Security obligations, federal "assets" will be sold— privatized—so in one stroke Social Security is phased out and privatization is phased in. The U.S. is on its way toward a free economy.

What about Medicare? Retirees pay only 25 percent of the program's costs through their premiums. In other words, the general public is subsidizing low-, middle-, and upper-income retirees. Upper-income retirees will have to bite the bullet and pay their own way. What is the income cutoff? $40,000 per year. Both middle-income and low-income retirees will strike a blow for family values. To make up the shortfall, the children and grandchildren of retirees will have to contribute to their parents, and grandparents' medical insurance premiums. (After all they are no longer paying $1.23 trillion in taxes, so they will have the ability to pay for the balance of the insurance premiums.) Instead of Social Security's potential generational warfare, this program will foster intergenerational harmony, concern, and compassion. (Now you can tell your parents and grandparents to get off the junk food, cut out their smoking, drink moderately, and get some exercise!) Organizations like AARP and other groups will then be in a position to negotiate with insurance companies, HMOs, hospitals, medical centers, nursing homes, etc., for the best possible health programs for their members. With more than 40 million current Social Security beneficiaries (and growing), there are plenty of senior citizen dollars to be spent on health care. Since consumers' dollars will be carefully spent, efficiency and quality must improve in the upcoming competition of a totally private health care market.

Retirees who cannot afford to pay all the insurance premiums may be taken on as indigent patients by health providers or subsidized by senior citizen organizations, unions, community groups, etc. The issue, therefore, is not if senior citizens will receive health care outside Medicare, but how. There is no limit to the possibilities; only the willingness to get government out of the health care business and construct an efficient high quality, low-cost health care delivery system. Asking the federal government to establish such a system is a trip to fantasyland. Government programs are neither high quality nor cost effective, so why bother trying to achieve the impossible?

The elimination of Medicaid would also lead to innovative programs at the local level to treat individuals who lack health insurance. Medicaid expenditures meanwhile will reach $96 billion in fiscal 1995, and is projected to climb to $136 billion in 1998, barring no changes in the Medicaid program. The amount needed to deliver health care to indigent citizens should decline dramatically because Medicaid will no longer be an open-ended entitlement, and poor people must make behavioral changes; otherwise the health care delivery system will be overwhelmed. In other words, a health care delivery system will be strained if consumers engage in activities that cause their health to deteriorate. The least expensive health care delivery system has been known for years: eat your vegetables, drink plenty of water, reduce saturated fat and cholesterol intake, don't smoke, drink moderately, exercise regularly, and eliminate stress. In addition, drinking and driving can be hazardous to your health, your fellow passengers, and others on the road. Annual checkups after the age of 40 should reduce the onset of major diseases quickly. To ignore the behavioral component of good health is to invite people to behave irresponsibly and then say to their fellow citizens, "You pay for our health care; it's our right."

In the 1990s, we are witnessing the logical result of government open-ended entitlements, particularly in the health care sector. Rather than face the reality of a failed program, public officials want to tinker with the present system which is unreformable, because it is premised on the entitlement philosophy. The next logical step from the public officials' perspective is to control medical fees and drug prices, and interfere with the suppliers of medical care. This is a typical bureaucratic response to a failed public policy, in this case blame the health care industry for the government's errors. (The Clinton health care proposal suggests a virtual government takeover of the health care system in the country. Don't buy it.)

The American people have been conditioned for more government control of a vital sector of the economy. Despite the skyrocketing health care costs associated government intervention over the past three decades, why do proponents of national health care assert that health care coverage will be less expensive with more government intervention? Health care can be delivered more efficiently when consumers have more choices in the marketplace and with $1.23 trillion in federal taxes eliminated. The consumer will be able to choose from a full menu offered by the health care industry. Moreover, every American will have an opportunity to participate, whether financially or by doing volunteer work, in delivering health care to both poor and low-income families. There will be no lack of goodwill on the part of the American people with the end of the Medicaid system, only the opposition from the collectivists who believe the government is the best institution for providing virtually all services in the economy, particularly health care.

National Security

The defense of the United States is the primary responsibility of the federal government. The defense budget can be reduced dramatically beginning immediately and reaching $150 billion by 1996–97. At that time, the military expenditures would reflect the minimum defense needs of the American people and not the alliances and interventionist policies which have proven so costly, both financially and in human lives, in the past. In the meantime, the cost of running the Defense Department, as well as other legitimate government functions, is estimated to be $260 billion. How would the revenue be raised in a tax-free America?

With a population of approximately 260 million and the initial cost of running the federal government nearly $260 billion, the per capita cost would be $1,000, a true egalitarian-democratic figure. Each American resident would pay a "head" fee to administer the federal government and be free from foreign aggression. But, such a payment schedule would impoverish low-income citizens. Yet, virtually all goods and services in the marketplace follow the law of one price. In other words, when consumers make purchases the sellers do not inquire about the income of the buyer and then price the good according to the ability to pay. The variety of goods in the marketplace makes it possible for all consumers regardless of income to satisfy their wants. However, when it comes to protection, upper- and middle-income individuals voluntarily pay much more than low-income families for burglar alarm systems to protect their valuable property. This notion is the basis for establishing a funding mechanism for national defense.

According to data available from the Internal Revenue Service, the American people paid $471 billion in personal income taxes in 1990. The IRS breakdown according to income categories is as follows:

Table 2

**Income Tax Paid in 1990 (in billions)
by Various Income Groups**

Income Group	Total Taxes Paid
Under $15,000	$16.4
$15,000-under $30,000	57.9
$30,000-under $50,000	96.1
$50,000-under $75,000	90.2
$75,000-under $100,000	46.8
$100,000-under $200,000	60.6
$200,000 and more	103.1

In order for a tax-free America to have the funds to pay for the legitimate functions of the federal government, Table 3 below contains a suggested fee schedule of the cost of being a U.S. citizen or resident. This fee schedule is the initial income needed to fund the federal government. In each income bracket the average fee has been multiplied by the number of exemptions, a rough approximation of the number of people in the United States. So, in each income bracket, individuals at the upper end would pay a little more while those at the lower end would pay slightly less. However, nothing prevents people from paying more than their "fair share." In fact, many individuals would undoubtedly pay more because of their desire to keep America free.

Businesses would chip in, too, but most corporations would pay little because they will need their $140 billion in taxes to fund their own research and development. The federal government's $76 billion R & D budget will be eliminated as part of the $500 billion reduction in so-called discretionary expenditures. In addition, corporations will be using some of their previous federal tax dollars for employee health care, family leave, day care, elder care, educational expenditures, etc. Anyone who doesn't pay the fee—the potential "free-rider"—would face enormous social pressure to pay his fair share. All employees will be asked to prove their contribution to the fund which could be certified by the Defense Department. Each individual would receive a card indicating in which fee bracket he contributed. Anyone not paying his share could be ostracized, not hired, or even fired. But as we saw in Chapter 2 wealthy individuals and businesses in ancient times supported public facilities, so the average citizen did not have to pay. In the following schedule, the liturgy is established in the United States. Individuals and businesses that contribute more than their "fair share" would reap benefits in the marketplace, greater sales, for example.

Table 3

Funding the Federal Government in Tax-Free America

Income Bracket	Average Per Capita Fee	Total Revenue
Under $15,000	$50-150	$3.0
15,000-under 30,000	300-500	27.0
30,000-under 50,000	750-1,250	58.0
50,000-under 75,000	1,300-2,000	52.0
75,000-under 100,000	2,200-2,700	30.0
100,000-under 200,000	3,000-7,500	42.0
200,000	12,000-25,000	48.0
		$244.4

Everyone in America will thus pay a share of the federal government's budget. In fact, every American family will pay a fraction of its current total liability to support the ultra-minimal government in Washington. Would this voluntary fee schedule work? If it doesn't, the American people would be demonstrating that they do not value their freedom and independence. This is doubtful, given the people's general support for a strong national defense. But, if the American people refuse to support the defense of the country, then they should learn one of several foreign languages and kiss their standard of living good-bye, because the United States would be ripe for an invasion from a potential aggressor. In a democracy, the people get the government they deserve. If the people "democratically" do not support a minimum national defense, then the American people will have demonstrated they prefer a little more money now than freedom and liberty for themselves and future generations. The American people are not stupid. They will not trade their standard of living and freedom for a few dollars more today.

Other Federal Spending

There is no perfect method to eliminate the federal government's role in the economy. The operating principle must be the sooner the better. Any initial "pain"—a few weeks or months—must not be a deterrent to establishing a sustainable, prosperous economy based on the economic principles many public officials and social scientists believe no longer are operable or work so poorly that only the government can straighten out the economy. The principles of the free market work fine.

By announcing the end of the federal leviathan one year (two years at most) in advance, nonprofit organizations will be able to gear up to meet the needs of individuals and families who require additional income assistance, medical care, counselling, training, and other programs to become productive, independent citizens. Some nonprofits will be eliminated because they are inefficient or duplicate the work of other better managed organizations in their areas. As Peter Drucker wrote, ". . . a well-managed nonprofit gets at least twice the bang out of each buck that a government agency does." But, he observes, "nonprofits have to learn how to raise money," because a "great many proprofits still believe that the way to get money is to hawk needs (emphasis in original)." Drucker's proposal to assist the nonprofits is to allow "taxpayers to deduct $1.10 for each dollar they give to nonprofits as a cash deduction." Drucker's $1.10 tax credit is a good beginning to phase in a tax-free America.

The $4 Trillion Plus Debt

The national debt is a disgrace! It is a result of decades of accelerating government expenditures without taxing the people to pay for them. Pay-as-you-go financing to pay for the welfare state would have lowered the American people's standard of living for decades, so the government instead borrowed and borrowed, and now the interest on the debt is the fastest increasing expenditure in the federal budget, and sucking up scarce capital that could be used by the private sector for the purchase of housing, automobiles, machines, factories, etc. The net interest on the debt is projected to be $212.8 billion in fiscal 1995, which exceeds the spending by the departments of agriculture, commerce, education, energy, interior, justice, state, and transportation plus the budgets of the National Aeronautics and Space Administration, Environmental Protection Agency, Congress, and the White House. There is only one immediate solution to the interest burden, a moratorium on interest payments. Whether the debt should be repaid is problematic.

A case can be made that after Social Security beneficiaries are paid off during the next several years, any remaining federal assets could be used to retire a portion of the debt.

But, given the elimination of all taxes—coerced levies—Americans who would have paid taxes in the future and currently hold U.S. government securities will, in effect, be losing their assets and interest payments in the meantime (government debt) but gaining future income—no taxes—so in less than a decade they probably will be no worse off. However, other assets will skyrocket in value, corporate bonds, real estate, and common stocks, because the federal government will be out of the capital markets, thus causing interest rates to decline. In addition, mortgage payments will probably plummet to the 4 percent level. Refinanced mortgages will save the American people tens of billions of dollars in annual interest charges. Thus, the American people will be much better off after a repudiation of all or most of the national debt. Moreover, such an act will prevent the government from borrowing in the future and preventing another transfer of wealth from the American people to government bondholders.

Sound Money and Banking

A tax-free America requires a money and banking system that does not lower the purchasing power of the monetary unit (inflation), that prevents any artificial stimulation of the economy (the boom) which then requires a period of adjustment (the bust), and that makes financial institutions subject to swift bankruptcy if it engages in unsound practices (fractional reserve banking). In addition, the people must disavow the notion that government sponsored bank "insurance" is an appropriate policy. Banking, like any other business, is risky and subject to failure. Banks can avoid potential losses and failures if they return to 100 percent reserves for their demand deposits and switch all their savings accounts into time accounts of various maturities, thirty to one hundred and twenty days and one to thirty years. Savers would deposit funds in accounts of varying maturity, just as they currently do when purchasing bonds. When a company's financial health declines and the bond's interest and/or principal are suspect, the bond's value falls. And, if the company should go under, the bondholders lose their capital; they are not insured against their loss. In other words, in a free market, risk is inherent in investing. This should be extended to the banking sector. Absence of government insurance would therefore cause bankers to be exceptionally prudent in their lending policies. Checking accounts would function as they currently do but subject to 100 percent reserve requirements in order to prevent monetary inflation by the banking system. This would be a major step toward financial discipline which would prevent banks from being subject to runs and massive losses. Moreover, the value of the depositors' savings certificates would fluctuate according to the health of the underlying borrowers. In other words, the banks would not be responsible for the payment of interest and/or principal on the certificates but would act as an intermediary between borrowers and lenders.

How could banks be profitable in such an environment? Would the public deposit their funds in uninsured savings accounts? Where would the money come from if the banks were not able to attract funds and lend them to businesses for working capital or capital goods purchases? How could people obtain mortgages if banks didn't have insured accounts? All valid questions, in an environment that has treated banks as special institutions protected by government. But, if the banking system's current structure is indeed sound, why does it need government insurance and protection? Because banks are unsound financial institutions, engines of inflation, aided and abetted by the granddaddy of inflation, the Federal Reserve with its unlimited checking account and "lender of last resort."

In a tax-free America, banks would be profitable or unprofitable depending on how well they manage the public's money entrusted to them. People will use banks if they believe the institutions are managed conservatively and efficiently. If banks make loans to businesses that fail at a higher rate than projected by the investment officers, then public confidence will drop as the depositors lose some of their money. Poorly managed banks will lose clients and either go out of business or be taken over by a better managed institution. Well-run banks will grow because they have managed their clients' funds without any or with minimal losses.

All banks will earn fees for their services, business and personal checking accounts, safe deposit services, brokerage services, wire transfers, travelers' checks, etc. In addition, they will originate personal loans, business loans, auto loans, residential and commercial mortgages, which may remain in the banks' portfolio or may be sold off in the secondary market to finance companies, pension funds, insurance companies, mutual funds, etc. In other words, banks will operate no different than today except there will be no government insurance, no federal or state bailout possible, and no inflating of the money supply.

To return to sound banking, the nation's monetary unit, the dollar, must once again be as good as gold, historically the world's preeminent monetary standard. In a commodity-based monetary system, all claims to real money, cash, and checking accounts must be redeemable in the metal—coins or bars—on demand. The Federal Reserve has approximately $11.059 billion worth of gold, which is valued at $42.22 per ounce. Based on these figures the Fed holds approximately 262 million ounces of the yellow metal. With the nation's basic money supply (cash and checkable deposits) approximately $1.1 trillion, the dollar can thus be defined as 1/4199 of an ounce of gold, a far cry from the definition of the dollar as 1/20 of an ounce of gold in 1792 or 1/35 an ounce in 1933.

In just the past decade, the supply of dollars has been greatly inflated. This indicates that massive monetary inflation occurred during the 1980s boom, which culminated in the recession of the late 1980s and early 1990s. Any citizen with

$4,199 would be able to obtain one ounce of gold from a bank. With banks having $54 billion in reserves, the Federal Reserve would redeem these dollars for gold as well as giving the banks a pro rata share of its gold hoard so the banks would be able to redeem all their checkable deposits and Federal Reserve currency for gold. The Federal Reserve would cease to exist. Its notes (paper money) would become bank notes and redeemable into gold at these institutions.[2] Its unlimited checking would be banished forever, and a free market money and banking system will have been established. Government monetary inflation would no longer be possible. Inflating the supply of credit would be possible but the banks would be subject to runs, thus making them shaky. The cycle of boom and bust would be ended, and prices would gently decline in the long run as the supply of goods would increase faster than the supply of new gold being extracted from mines around the world. Interest rates would decline as inflationary expectations disappear. Savings and investment would increase as both borrowers and lenders had confidence in the integrity of the monetary unit and in the stability of interest rates. The U.S. economy would attract capital from all over the world if it unilaterally reimposed the gold standard, or the world economy would enjoy a global boom if all nations reformed their monetary systems and banking institutions.

The end of "trickle-down" economics would finally occur, from the Fed to bankers, to corporations, to their employees, to merchants, to fixed-income households, to the poor. Our current monetary system epitomizes trickle-down economics, a process that injects money into the economy benefitting upper income households first and then trickling down to the masses. In addition, monetary inflation redistributes income and wealth from the low-income families up the economic ladder, to the wealthiest sectors of the economy. Ludwig von Mises succinctly describes the redistribution of income.

While inflation is under way, some people enjoy the benefit of higher prices for the goods or services they sell, while the prices for goods and services they buy have not yet risen or have not risen to the same extent. These people profit from their fortunate position. Inflation seems to them "good business" a "boom". But their gains are always derived from the losses of other sections of the population. The losers are those in the unhappy situation of selling services or commodities whose prices have not yet risen to the same degree as have prices of the things they buy for daily consumption.[3]

The chains of monetary bondage will finally be broken when money is separated from government. A new golden age of production, investment, and consumption will be ushered in when real money will replace the government's funny money, ending the redistribution of wealth and income. Instead of the Federal Reserve destabilizing the economy by inflating and deflating the supply of money and credit, the natural workings of the free market will allocate resources to their most highly valued uses. Government will play an important role in the economy, assuring market participants that actions threatening the territorial integrity of the United States will be repelled and that local governments' highest priority will be ensuring domestic tranquility.

The States

What should the states do in a tax-free America? Historically, state governments have been involved in transportation projects, canals, turnpikes, railroads, and highways. Although their constitutions have mandated public education, it was generally left to municipalities to build and staff schools, with the state providing some aid from sales and income taxes. Local schools have been generally funded by a combination of local property taxes and state aid. In recent years, federal aid has been available for urban school districts and suburban districts that qualify.

To highlight what one state believes it should do, excerpts from New Jersey's 1992–93 budget is instructive. Governor Florio early in his message to the Legislature states: "Government can't do everything. But if opportunity is on the second floor and people are on the first floor, government can be the ladder and it should." Nowhere does the governor explain why opportunity is on the second floor. "Opportunity" is all around us; insight separates people who wait for opportunity to "knock" on their door and those who "seize the moment" because they see an opportunity in society. What prevents people from seeking an opportunity is the numerous barriers government erects in the path of individuals who have the desire but not the financial ability to overcome the regulatory burdens placed on small and medium-sized business. One brief example is the low-cost day care that could be offered by some women in their home for working couples and single parents but cannot because of state licensing regulations. As a true "cottage" industry, the state requires several health and safety criteria that cannot be met by these fledgling entrepreneurs, and municipalities routinely prevent such activities in residential neighborhoods. The upshot, parents cannot obtain affordable day care, new businesses are not started, and the call is heard, "See, the private sector cannot provide day care, we need a government day care policy." This statement is yet another example of collectivist thinking that permeates our society.

Throughout his budget Governor Florio lists what the state should do. A brief excerpt of the hundreds of state government activities include:

• To expand domestic and foreign markets for New Jersey agricultural products.

• To promote direct farmer-to-consumer sales.

• To retain a healthy economic environment for a viable, competitive dairy industry where farmers are assured a fair return for milk sold to processors; consumers are assured adequate supplies of milk at the lowest possible prices.

•To provide non-commercial educational television or radio services to New Jersey's citizens.

•To promote the expansion and growth of commerce, industry and tourism in order to increase employment in New Jersey.

•To collect, analyze and disseminate economic data for the benefit of business and industry located within the state.

•To promote and assist businesses and industries, to export and to encourage foreign investment in New Jersey.

•To promote further development of New Jersey's academic research capabilities in priority fields, and to identify and evaluate new fields of opportunity.

•To provide for the protection of the health, safety, welfare, and rights of the residents of the State's rooming and boarding homes.

•To preserve the existing multi-family housing stock in the state and protect the health and safety of the occupants.

•To provide federal rental assistance payments to low income families and rehabilitation of existing housing units, with a special emphasis on services to the mentally and physically handicapped.

•To promote and encourage advocacy for the aging population at the federal, State, county and municipal levels in order to ensure that the elderly will not be deprived of their rights, privileges, entitlements, or benefits.

•To provide financial assistance to all public local education agencies for operating costs.

•To provide financial assistance for the education of children attending non-public schools.

•To support the State's workforce readiness system by providing quality programs responsive to the needs of both workers and employers, expanding occupational education programs that appropriately prepare individuals for work in all types of education.

•To collect and maintain library resources and to provide information and other library services to State government employees and the general public; and, the statewide library network, to provide or locate needed supplementary information or materials not available to patrons at their local libraries.

•To provide clean and safe recreational, historic, natural and interpretative facilities.

•To protect the public and the environment against unnecessary radiation exposure from natural and man-made sources.

•To remediate sites contaminated by man-made hazardous substances and pollutants for the benefit of human health and to restore contaminated areas of the state for beneficial use.

•To provide a comprehensive energy supply and demand strategy that allows for responsible and necessary growth and development without compromising the environment and quality of life in New Jersey.

•To reduce infant mortality and improve the health of mothers and children. . .

•To ensure high quality health care accessible to all New Jerseyans, in a safe environment . . . at reasonable costs . . .

•To improve and expand statewide planning efforts in order to maintain a rational basis for institutional and programmatic development in higher education.

•To develop a comprehensive range of accessible, coordinated mental health services for all citizens of the state, with emphasis on the development of local mental health programs.

•To establish, maintain and supervise an effective public assistance system, ensuring the uniform administration of income maintenance programs in compliance with Federal and State statues and regulations.

•To prevent employment practices which are injurious to workers or which abrogate worker's rights and to assure equitable wages and working hours.

•To assure fair, equitable and competent treatment of the consumer in practices relating to the acquisition of goods and services, and the use of professional and occupational services.

•To increase public participation in the arts, develop audience education in the arts, increase total artistic resources, and increase the availability of professional training in the arts.

•To maintain State roads, bridges and railroad properties, and to ensure safe and efficient movement of traffic.

•To provide a capital planning process within which the State's human economic and physical resources can be developed and utilized in an effective manner.

Although Governor Florio stated the government cannot do everything, it isn't from a lack of trying. There is virtually no sector of the economy and society untouched by state government, and New Jersey is undoubtedly not alone in its commitment to economic development, health, education, welfare, housing, transportation, the arts, environmental protection, employer-employee relations, consumer protection, the elderly, and recreation facilities. Of course, the state government has a vital role in maintaining law and order and punishing offenders; that goes without saying. For, keeping the peace and administering justice are the primary responsibility of all governments. Yet, state government has stepped beyond its bounds when it began to intervene massively in the economy.

The list of activities the state undertakes is well beyond what government should do. With such commitments expressed in the state budget, the government has to tax the citizens' personal income, their purchases (sales tax), and businesses to pay for the expenditures. When the government spends, the public has to spend and invest less, reducing their present and future living standards. The state thus engages in a substantial transfer of wealth and some of the beneficiaries are upper-income families (boat owners, for example) and business owners (dairy farmers, exporters, and others). If the benefits received are greater than what the beneficiaries pay in taxes, they are receiving a subsidy. If the benefits received are less than they pay in taxes then what they are being plundered. But, the same problem exists at the state level that exists at any other level of government: What are these benefits worth? Without a market for all goods and services the "value" of the state's expenditures are arbitrary at best. We know the cost of the state's expenditures but not their value. The solution, therefore, is to place these activities in the non-public sector. Otherwise, the government's activities will remain politicized—the vying for funds by lobbies who claim to have a right to the public's money. Each year the budget battle

becomes more acrimonious because there are more demands
for the public's dollars while the productive sector's growth is
hampered because of excessive regulation and higher taxes.
As Paul Tsongas stated during the 1992 presidential primaries,
"You cannot love jobs and hate employers." Abolishing taxes
and eliminating virtually all regulations, except rules against
force and fraud, will do more to spur economic growth and job
creation than all targeted tax cuts and government subsidies.
In a tax-free society, the "playing field" will be level, with no
subsidies or special privileges transferring wealth from one
individual to another or one group to another group.

The defeat of Governor Florio by Christine Todd
Whitman in November 1993 is instructive. Mrs. Whitman
promised a 30 percent reduction in the state's income tax
during the campaign as well as an overhaul of state spending.
Although ridiculed by the press and the former governor, Mrs.
Whitman defeated an incumbent who substantially raised
taxes early in his term. It remains to be seen how successful
Governor Whitman will be in reducing the role of the state in
New Jersey's economy during the next several years.

Counties and Municipalities

Counties and municipalities undertake many activities including airport operations, educational and hospital
services, drug and alcohol abuse programs, water sewer, and
transit services, welfare assistance, housing development,
building and maintaining streets, roads and highways, providing recreational facilities, police protection, court system, and
solid waste collection facilities to name just the most well-
known services. Yet, the public's satisfaction with the
government's delivery of these services is far from overwhelming. In fact, virtually every service local governments
deliver has been criticized by both proponents and critics of
governmental involvement in the economy. With such a

backdrop, plus the fiscal squeeze local governments currently face, government "closest to the people" must be refocused to provide a framework so all citizens can have the services they want delivered as effectively as possible. These services would include those which have traditionally been thought to be exclusively governmentally or partially governmentally delivered—schools, streets and highways, parks and recreation, hospitals, housing, refuse collection, mass transit, and welfare assistance. Even police protection and the court system, which very few analysts believe should be "privatized" has, in recent years, seen some of its responsibilities handled by private firms or nonprofit and voluntary associations. Block patrols, private security guards for public facilities, private arbitration and mediation, and other services demonstrate that even the peacekeeping function and the settling of disputes can be handled outside traditional public sector institutions.

For every public sector institution delivering services to the people there is a counterpart in the nonpublic sector. Although some of these nonprofit organizations receive public funds to carry out their activities, the administration of the public monies requires a government bureaucracy which does not deliver any services. Government, therefore, wastes huge sums of money in addition to engaging in legal plunder, all in the name of helping people. The task, therefore, is not if governmentally delivered services can be provided by the profit and nonprofit sectors, but do we, as a people, have the courage to eliminate both legal plunder and inefficiency and establish an economy based on sound economic principles? Or, do we want to continue engaging in a peaceful, ongoing "civil war" known as the annual governmental budget? The former leads to a harmonious, prosperous society based on fundamental economic principles and noncoercive interpersonal relations, while the latter leads to social strife and economic stagnation. We are in the latter stages of our civil

war. If government intervention is not reduced and government does not return to its most important function in society,
more strife and greater impoverishment will occur. The people
must choose wisely; the stakes are indeed very high.

8

Timetable for a Tax-Free America

Liberty...has the potential for appealing to all groups across the public spectrum. Yet, it is a fact of life that when things are going smoothly, most people fail to develop any interest in public affairs. For radical social change—a change to a different social system—to take place there must be what is called a "crisis situation."

--Murray Rothbard

Do we need a "crisis" to transform the U. S. from a quasi-socialized economy to a free economy? Or, can we have a smooth transition to a *laissez-faire* economy. Whether we have a crisis or not, the American people must first realize why America is a shell of its former greatness. The American people need to understand that the American dream—limited government at home, the dollar as "good as gold," and peaceful relations with all nations—is but a memory. We can do something about it!

Tax-Free 2000 will become a reality when the people realize that the spider web theory of government must be abolished. James Payne describes the process but does not name it explicitly.

Year by year, governments increase the number of citizens they subsidize. The poor were one of the first groups to be targeted, then came the elderly, then farmers, then the unemployed, then small businessmen, then college students, then

scientists, then composers. Today, it is difficult to find an
economic sector or population group that government does not
subsidize.[1]

Also included in the government's web is the banking
system, and its depositors. In addition, corporations receive
research grants, foreign customers of U. S. corporations
receive subsidized loans and occasionally U.S. corporations
get a federal bailout, e.g., Chrysler. Another interest group is
the states and cities, which depend on federal aid for their
spending programs. With such a formidable array of interest
groups, it is no mystery that the government's spider web has
turned the American people into a nation of addicts, addicted
to other people's money. However, Payne extends his analysis to the most critical element of government taxation and
spending that is either ignored or not understood (let's give
them the benefit of the doubt) by the proponents of statism.

> Unfortunately, the funds for all these helping programs do
> not come from the sky. The wealth the federal government
> disposes comes from the citizens themselves. Therefore, as
> government expands the size and number of its helping pro-
> grams, it is bound to get into a situation where it is taxing the
> same people it is trying to help in its subsidy programs.[2]

You do not have to be a rocket scientist to realize that
taxation and spending are nothing more than a gigantic
transfer of money from the people to the government and back
to the people, leaving the people worse off! (Of course,
subsidies do exist, that is, getting more in tax dollars than you
pay in taxes. But, this needs to be studied on a case-by-case
basis and is beyond the scope of this study.) Once this lesson
is learned and embraced by the American people, a tax-free
America will be born and the semi-socialistic U.S. economy
will be eliminated once and for all.

How socialized is the U.S. economy? According to the 1995 federal budget submitted by President Clinton in February 1994, the federal government will spend approximately $1.5 trillion in the fiscal year that ends on 30 September 1995, or roughly $6,000 per capita. Federal spending will comprise approximately 25 percent of the nations $6 trillion Gross Domestic Product (GDP). But, the federal government's share of the productive economy is understated because GDP includes government spending, so if we exclude federal outlays a different picture emerges.

Federal government outlays should be considered a burden on the economy because it represents coerced spending, and therefore the government's activities cause the output of goods and services to be different than if the United States had a free market. The only exception would be legitimate and necessary national defense expenditures, but here, too, the appropriate amount the people would want to spend cannot be determined because of taxation. Because the federal government's "web," as Payne so clearly describes, covers virtually all sectors of the economy, it is difficult to arrive at a precise figure of the federal government's exact burden on the U.S. economy, especially when the regulatory costs are estimated between $430 to $562 billion. Supposedly, Americans benefit from these regulations, obtaining more health and safe working conditions and less pollution. But, the bottom line, according to some analysts, is that all levels of government take and control about 60 percent of the national output.

The federal government's $1.5 trillion budget is spread among the following categories:

Table 4

**Projected Federal Government Outlays
for Fiscal 1995**
(in billions of dollars)

National Defense	$270.7
International Affairs	17.8
General Science, Space & Technology	16.9
Energy	4.6
Natural Resources & Environment	21.8
Agriculture	12.8
Transportation	38.4
Community & Regional Development	9.2
Education, Training, Employment & Social Services	53.5
Health	123.1
Medicare	156.2
Income Security	221.4
Social Security	337.2
Veterans Benefits and Services	39.2
Administration of Justice	17.3
General Government	13.8
Net Interest	212.8

Within each federal program, there are categories, sub-categories, and sub-sub-categories. Thus, taxes are "chewed up" by Washington's bureaucracies, leaving taxpayers in general worse off. As Payne so eloquently describes this transfer scheme.

> If you take $1.00 from a farmer in taxes and then give him back $1.10 in various benefit programs, the assumption is that he is 10 cents to the good, and the rest of the world is unaffected.
>
> Once we include the real-world costs of operating the transfer system, we see how destructive the pattern of self-subsidy can be—even to targeted beneficiaries. If, in the above illustration, the true cost to the farmers of paying $1.00 in taxes

is actually $1.65 (owing to his tax-compliance burden, its incentive effects, etc.), then the tax subsidy system leaves him a net loser to the tune of 55 cents to the dollar. And everyone else who has paid taxes to fund the farm subsidy is a total loser, bearing both the tax burden and the tax system cost.[3]

Examining the federal government's outlays, there are only a few categories that benefit all Americans—national defense, state department functions, general government, and the administration of justice. But, even in these programs, there are outlays which subsidize other countries, e.g., U.S. troops overseas and foreign aid (both military grants and economic assistance), and expenditures that have dubious value to all the American people. All other spending programs are examples of money flowing from the people to Washington back to some of the people. These programs must be terminated, eliminating the deadweight of Washington's bureaucracies, so the economy can grow naturally.

One example of the dozens of spending programs on the budget highlights Payne's thesis about taxes, spending, and subsidies. The Agricultural program will spend $10.1 billion on what is called "Farm Income Stabilization." If farmers pay $10.1 billion in federal taxes they are receiving in effect their own money. If they pay less than $10.1 billion in federal taxes then they are being subsidized by the rest of the population and are the recipients of legal plunder. In either case, the government's agricultural programs are unnecessary at best and harmful at worst. Moreover, as Payne's analysis clearly demonstrates, the benefits received by recipients are much less than the taxes they pay. Subsidizing farmers, therefore, some of whom are large corporations, is yet another example of how the welfare state benefits big business. What justification is there for such highway robbery? None! Although central planning is considered a foreign, alien practice, the federal government's budget projections are, in fact, no different from any socialist country's multi-year plan.

In program after program, housing, transportation, community development, health care, education, space exploration, natural resources, and the environment, the federal government is distorting the marketplace, and shifting funds to satisfy both the bureaucrats and special interests' objectives at the expense of the vast majority of the American people. Instead of the marketplace (people buying and selling goods and services reflecting their desires) determining the allocation of resources, the federal government's web determines to a great degree how Americans should live. The federal government's spending programs, therefore, are both anti-producer and anti-consumer. Thus, the assets—buildings, installations, land, etc.,—under the federal government's control must be disgorged and sold off to the highest bidders so the revenue can be used to phase out Social Security and other "contractual" spending. This action will free up the people's income and the federal government's assets to the productive sector (profit and nonprofit organizations) in order to eliminate the distorting effect of politics on the allocation of resources.

Downsizing Government

A phase out of Social Security was briefly discussed in the last chapter but several details of how the process will leave no one worse off were omitted. The data below reveal that not only will Social Security recipients be no worse off but most recipients will be better off in a tax-free America.

According to economist Neil Howe's policy paper, *Controlling Entitlements: The Argument for Comprehensive "Means-Testing"* published by the National Taxpayers Union foundation (April 22, 1992), Social Security recipients, including those receiving disability payments, in 1991 obtained the following funds (by family income) from the federal government.

Table 5

**Federal Budget Outlays for Social Security Recipients
1991**
(in billions of dollars)

Family Income	Social Security	Medicare
Under $10,000	$38.82	$19.78
$10,000-$20,000	64.91	24.82
$20,000-$30,000	53.48	19.07
$30,000-$50,000	63.71	21.94
$50,000-$100,000	41.34	14.28
Over $100,000	13.95	4.68
	$275.72	$104.57

Social Security old-age beneficiaries and citizens getting disability payments thus received $380 billion in 1991. Another table reveals the actual average benefit per household from Social Security and Medicare.

Table 6

**Federal Social Security and Medicare Benefits
per Household**

Recipient Household Only	Social Security	Medicare
Under $10,000	$6,461	$3,538
$10,000–$20,000	9,902	4,224
$20,000–$30,000	11,438	4,589
$30,000–$50,000	11,988	4,664
$50,000–$100,000	11,789	4,650
Over $100,000	13,966	4,602

Households in the over $100,000 category pay for their own benefits with a combination of their federal, state, and local taxes. In a tax-free America there would be no state and local taxes either, so these windfalls (the abolition of these taxes) mean more Social Security recipients would have lower tax liabilities. Therefore, their benefits should be adjusted downward accordingly. For example, if a couple has a $100,000 household income and pays approximately $20,000 in federal taxes, $3,000 in state taxes, $6,000 in property taxes ($4,000 of which pays for public schools, the remaining $2,000 for police, sanitation, sewers, roads, etc.,) Abolishing all taxes except those levies that are necessary to provide such services as local roads, sewers, police, etc., would save them $27,000 per year. Eliminating the approximately $19,000 they receive in federal benefits would leave them ahead by $8,000. However, the couple would still have to contribute to the national defense, let's say $5,000 to $8,000. This hypothetical couple with an income of $100,000 would at worst break even. The implication of the above data suggest that Social Security recipients, especially those with incomes above $50,000, would pay for their own benefits. Households with incomes in the $30,000 to $50,000 range also pay substantial federal, state, and local taxes. With the federal government's assets valued more than $5 trillion, even if Social Security recipients, after deducting their tax liabilities from their benefits, require $250 billion per year, the federal government has more than enough assets to pay off present and future beneficiaries. Moreover, the economic benefits of a tax-free America will increase the beneficiaries' wealth as common stocks, corporate bonds, real estate, etc. appreciate, so that whatever losses they will suffer because of the partial or total national debt repudiation, will more than be made up by this overhaul of the government's finances and restructuring of the economy.

Low-income families would receive the difference between their stated retirement benefit and any taxes they would have paid. So, if a couple receives $6,000 in yearly benefits and pays $1,000 in taxes, they would now receive $5,000 in benefits. The couple's Medicare coverage would be canceled and picked up by their children and/or grandchildren, whose taxes have been abolished, thereby increasing their annual incomes. If for some reason the children and/or grandchildren do not assist their parents and grandparents, a highly unlikely prospect, a safety valve method to fund Medicare and other benefits such as disability insurance, supplemental security income (SSI) and veterans benefits, would be a national lottery. A national lottery could generate billions of dollars annually. If every adult on average would spend $10 per month that would generate at least $1.5 to $2.0 billion or $18 to $36 billion per year. With prizes and expenditures totaling $8 to $14 billion, $10 to $20 billion could be raised, which would be used by retirees to purchase their own medical insurance and the very poor retirees and disabled to obtain some income. In addition, nonprofit agencies would pick up some of the costs as well as other organizations, unions, businesses, clinics, etc. There is no lack of goodwill in America; just ask the people of south Florida, whose communities were destroyed by Hurricane Andrew.

Phasing out the federal government's entitlement programs will cement family relationships. Parents will be paying for their children's education and upbringing and their children will assist their parents when they retire. Generational bonds will be strengthened in a tax-free America, unlike today when the elderly are considered burdens, and off they go to the nursing home.

What are the pitfalls to this phaseout? Some retirees may shift assets to children, grandchildren, or organizations in order to reduce their reported income so they would not lose any Social Security benefits. Because the phasing out of Social Security will benefit all the American people, such an act would be a severe breach of trust. Consequently, every retiree must continue to file a 1040 return, not with the IRS, but with the Social Security Administration, and any asset shifting will result in the immediate termination of all Social Security payments. In other words, the plan calls for the highest ethical conduct on the part of the American people and attempts to take advantage of any uncertainty during the transition must be dealt with severely.

What if retirees had planned to make gifts to their children, grandchildren, other relatives, and organizations over the next several years? This is more problematic since these bequests would reduce the retirees' income and necessitate higher Social Security payments, when the goal is to reduce the monthly and annual outlays. If these couples or individuals make sizeable donations or gifts, lowering their taxes below their Social Security income, that is their choice but it will not trigger higher Social Security payments. Other retirees, for example, who receive $1,000 per month from Social Security have few assets so the tax liability will be nonexistent because of the standard deduction, exemptions, etc. Thus, no higher payments will be triggered. What may seem like a hurdle will not materialize because senior citizens are treated relatively well by the current tax code, e.g., double personal exemptions.

A possible stumbling block is the soon-to-be retirees. There must be a cutoff age, perhaps fifty-five, that would be the dividing line between those (under fifty-five) who will not receive any Social Security payments in the future and future retirees who will receive a scaled-back benefit schedule. The idea behind this proposal is straightforward. With no taxes to pay, individuals will be able to save for their retirement so they can retire at age sixty-two, sixty-five, sixty-eight, etc., with substantial investment funds. In short, with the elimination of Social Security taxes, employees will be able to accumulate, in addition to any current company pension, 401(k) or IRA contributions, a new tax-free pension plan, which will grow substantially. Finally, Americans will be able to have sound retirement plans based on saving and investing in U.S. and/or overseas businesses. This will generate one of the greatest bursts of productivity the world has ever seen. That's a 24-karat gold guarantee!

States, Counties, and Municipalities

If New Jersey's state budget is typical of the remaining forty-nine states, then state governments have bitten off more than they can chew. The notion that government must educate the young, provide health care, assist the poor, and promote businesses, etc., begs the question, how is government to pay for these services? If government—state, county, or local— wants to construct facilities to carry out these services, then a noncoercive method must be found, otherwise legal plunder will occur. As noble as the goals of the government's programs may be, the manner in which the government is financed is just as important as the objective. Creating a just society means establishing liberty and prosperity. Prosperity is the result of free people making exchanges so both the buyer and seller can be better off. As the Great Seal of the State of New Jersey attests, liberty and prosperity are the state's tradition. The state budget belies that honorable idea. To reestablish Liberty and Prosperity in New Jersey as well as in the other forty-nine states, enacting the following general principles will boost the economy and the nonprofit sector so they can meet the people's genuine needs.

Using New Jersey as the model, states must withdraw from all sectors of the economy that do not involve police protection and the administration of justice. Even at the state level, the corrections budget could be scaled back dramatically. Individuals convicted of violent crimes, murder, rape and robbery, etc., and those convicted of other crimes, theft, burglary, etc., must continue to serve their time in prison. Serious consideration should be given, however, to relying less on prisons for nonviolent criminals, and using other methods, e.g., restitution and community service. As far as individuals convicted of violent crimes in the future are concerned, we should give serious consideration to revoking the citizenship of violent felons. This means deporting them to their ancestral homes or uncharted territories around the world. Another possibility is paying nations a one-time fee, say $10,000 to $20,000 to accept these criminals for labor in their societies. The Russians could use tens of millions of dollars. Accepting a few thousand felons who could be utilized to work in Siberia would solve our problem with felons and the Russians' need for "rugged" laborers. It's a win-win situation. While this may seem harsh, individuals who kill or rape violate the basic tenets of a civilized society—they continue to aggress against their fellow citizens.

Banishment is a humane treatment for both murderers and individuals who have committed savage assaults. Violent crime is undermining social stability and the only way besides capital punishment to permanently remove dangerous convicts is to revoke their citizenship and deport them far, far away. The American people must thus make a fundamental choice, continue to pay for prisons where convicts earn doctorates in criminal behavior, or remove the criminals from civilized society, by expressing their disgust and revulsion against violent behavior.

The government's welfare system must be abolished. Ending welfare will be a blessing for both recipients and the public. But, without taxes and government programs, how will the "deserving" poor obtain food, clothing, shelter, and the medical care they need? Eliminating the welfare bureaucracies will save billions of dollars nationwide. During the transition, however, before the government's complete withdrawal from welfare, a nationwide summit of all county-based nonprofit agencies will meet in their respective states to plan a strategy for a tax-free America. With the assistance of management experts, each county's social services agencies will meet to discuss priority needs in their area, e.g., housing, job training, food assistance, and medical care, to identify the families that need assistance, to coordinate their programs efficiently, and to plan fundraising strategies. The new welfare system will be tailored for each community so innovative programs can be implemented without legal impediments and delays from Washington or the state capitals.

The transition period must be no longer than two years. During the transition Drucker's $1.10 tax credit for every $1.00 contributed could be implemented at the state level so the "spirit of giving" expands. During the transition, local nonprofits will be receiving more revenue and their programs will expand while the government's programs will be phased out. By the time government programs are abolished, the nonprofits will have taken over social services throughout the county. Instead of receiving money, food stamps, and housing unconditionally, the new welfare system should demand some work in return for benefits. The work could be in a hospital, day care center, nursing home, drug and alcohol rehabilitation center, medical clinic, school, etc.

A medical care program could be modeled after Dr. Joe Greer's efforts in Miami. He was profiled on ABC News on 20 November 1992 as "Person of the Week." Dr. Greer treats the homeless in Miami and teaches at one of the local medical colleges. He stated he has a responsibility, not a legal obligation, to treat the less fortunate in his area. Programs throughout the country based on Dr. Greer's heroic efforts could be the prototype of treating the poor in a tax-free America. Also, welfare recipients must enroll in a job training program, one of which could be established by a consortium of corporations in each county or every state. Inasmuch as business taxes will have been eliminated, some of the funds could be used for teaching basic reading and writing and new technical skills to current welfare recipients.

There is no lack of imaginative programs in the nonprofit sector to assist poor and low-income citizens to become productive and independent. The country needs a philosophical overhaul, beginning with the notion that people's needs are

other people's legal obligations. Once this untenable philosophical proposition is discarded the American people can
begin to assist each other humanely. The current welfare
system breeds contempt for the poor, breaks up families, and
fosters dependency. The welfare system in a tax-free American will do just the opposite: it will treat the poor with dignity
and respect, strengthen families, and create more independent
households. The country can bank on it!

Public schools will become profit or nonprofit institutions in a tax-free America. Abolishing the state and county
education's bureaucracies will lower the cost per pupil. Stream-
lining each school's administrative staff will further reduce
costs. With a reduction in bureaucracies, schools will be able
to offer higher pay to attract and keep the best teachers.
Transforming the current politicized system to a nongovernmental setting will be fiercely challenged by the National
Education Association and the American Federation of Teachers. But, the rank and file teacher should welcome nongovernmental schools because professionalism will replace the civil
service mentality—"equal pay for unequal work." Teachers
will be paid according to seniority in some schools, according
to special skills they possess or strictly according to their
teaching effectiveness. In every profession except teaching,
the practitioners earn their income based on their skills and
output. Lawyers, doctors, accountants, engineers, etc., earn
their income because they have satisfied clients, while teachers are currently paid because of a contractual agreement
having nothing to do with the teachers' effectiveness, but
primarily on his or her longevity. Excellent public school
teachers, in effect, are subsidizing their incompetent "brothers
and sisters." In a nonpublic educational system, the owners or
trustees of the schools have a moral and fiduciary responsibility to hire the best teachers and fire or retrain the incompetent

ones. Abolishing public education will make teaching a profession, instead of just a civil service position, twenty years (or age 55) and out.

Reforming education begins with putting public education on a user fee basis. This immediately would put the educational establishment on a sound financial foundation. Parents will now pay for their children's education and thus will be very concerned about the local school's cost structure, inasmuch as there will be no subsidies from other property owners, singles, childless couples, senior citizens, and businesses. The end of the federal income tax will increase after-tax income of households with children so they will be able to pay for the education bill. In the suburbs this should not pose a problem. The more difficult school finances to be resolved will occur in urban areas where the majority of America's poor and low-income families live. During the transition, urban schools will be supported by tuition (to be determined by each urban district), foundations, grants from businesses, fund-raising, etc. Currently, schools are closely involved with corporations throughout the county, according to *Fortune* (November 16, 1992). A who's who of American businesses contribute hundreds of millions of dollars to schools, in addition to the taxes they pay. Eliminating federal and state taxes would free up not only the direct tax payments but also the funds corporations use to collect data and analyze statistics relating to the tax compliance process. These funds could be shifted to education and other productive uses. There is, therefore, not a lack of money to fund a first-class educational system, but a misallocation of resources and a highly politicized, bureaucratic structure is in place. A nonpublic educational system will thus be "consumer driven," instead of bureaucratically driven, involving parents more closely in their children's educational progress because their money will be at stake, not the "government's" (i.e., all taxpayers).

During the transition, local governments will have to negotiate with parents, teachers, and administrators about transforming the schools from a public entity into a nonprofit-or-profit oriented institution. Most schools will probably become nonprofit, initially because there may not be enough investors to purchase the schools. However, corporations, parent-teacher organizations, foundations, and other interested parties may operate a school or schools jointly. If the schools will be operated on a nonprofit basis, the physical facilities should be transferred to the nonprofit corporation with a proviso that it would have to run as a nonprofit for at least twenty years, for example. If the school or schools become a profit oriented facility, then the owners would have to make a contribution to the municipality to help pay off any local government debt outstanding or assist more in the education of recipients, if there are any remaining. If an investor group, a corporation, or syndicate wants to obtain a school, it should purchase the facilities at a slight discount from an objective market assessment of the school's value. The proceeds could retire local debt or be used to distribute to the area's taxpayers.

The schools' structure in a tax-free America would reflect the parents' and their children's educational needs. Statewide curricula or even national educational goals would be scrapped in favor of decentralized, entrepreneurially driven educational facilities. Bright college students would now view teaching as a first choice career opportunity rather than a job they could fall back on if other opportunities were not available. Higher pay and better working conditions would make education one of the most desirable professional career choices. "Special needs" educational institutions for physically and emotionally disabled children will have to become entrepreneurial like other nonprofit facilities in society.

Public colleges and universities will become private nonprofit institutions, funded by tuition, endowments, fundraisers, lotteries, etc. Some students could work in the college to help defray expenses. Local businesses will undoubtedly increase their contributions for capital projects and operating expenses. Banks could offer subsidized loans to students and their families, instead of the government subsidizing college education. In short, there would be sufficient ideas to fund college education in a tax-free America. The only opposition would come from students, college administrators, and professors who believe that higher education is a right and that taxpayers should foot the bill. Although students have the right to pursue higher education, they do not have the right to expect their fellow citizens to subsidize them. In fact, in a tax-free America students, employed full- or part-time, will not have to pay taxes subsidizing other citizens, so there should be no hardship for hardworking students to pay for most or all of their college education.

Roads, highways, water, and sewers could be "privatized" as nonprofit organizations, but most likely should become profit-oriented facilities. These facilities could be sold to the highest bidder or sold at a deep discount so a market return on equity could be achieved. Otherwise, no investors will bid for the properties. During the transition then, gasoline taxes (user fees) and other charges would remain in order for the public sector to have sufficient revenue to cover the costs of operation. But, the public sector's operations of roads, highways, bridges, water-sewer facilities, and mass transit, suffer from one great flaw—massive subsidies. If a service cannot be delivered without subsidies then there is a gross misallocation of resources. Either the cost structure is too high or the user fee, if any, is too low. In some cases, there are no user fees, with operating funds coming from general tax revenues. The method is inefficient and breeds corruption. The history of urban America is one of bribes and payoffs to obtain lucrative contracts for water and sewer systems, parking facilities and transportation operations. Moreover, without the private ownership of assets, public sector accountability is an exercise in faith because the firing of incompetent officials and employees is a difficult but not impossible process. The public is thus stuck with the local administration hiring different officials who promise to clean up the mess of their predecessors. Meanwhile, service deteriorates, taxes rise, and the public suffers. There has to be a better way. There is—the transfer of assets to profit or nonprofit organizations with competent managers and employees. The frustrated, qualified employees in the public sector will be absorbed in these organizations while the political hacks and incompetent employees will have to shape up in a new line of work. The taxpayers will be liberated once and for all.

Unemployment insurance, health and safety regulations will be decentralized and standards will be established by businesses, their employees and representatives in a tax-free America. The operation of each corporation and industry must be handled by the owners and their employees. Each industry has different requirements and bureaucratic standards raise costs and impede innovative solutions. Private certifying agencies such as Underwriters Laboratory could do for the workplace what is already being done for products. Liability for an unsafe work environment must rest with the owners of the business and not be socialized through government programs. Overhauling the regulations and programs governing the health and safety of the American worker will lead to safer conditions because government standards tend to become the minimum conditions employers meet and because they have no incentive to improve the workplace environment. If employers meet the legal minimum safety requirements, then competitive pressures will force them not to exceed them because there is no advantage. But, in a decentralized system, a safer environment will lower insurance rates for corporations and attract more productive workers, boosting profits. Corporations that have lax safety standards in tax-free America will have higher insurance premiums, greater "down time" on the production line and an exodus of their best workers. In addition, corporations with poor safety records will undoubtedly be subject to consumer boycotts.

The risk of unemployment will be desocialized in tax-free America. Insuring unemployment will be handled through unions, professional organizations, employer-employee joint efforts, but not through the tax system. The possibility of unemployment will increase savings, the proverbial rainy day fund for emergencies. Consequently, more funds will become available for capital formation. But in tax-free America, all unemployment will be temporary because there will be no systematic economic downturn causing massive layoffs. In addition, unemployment compensation is a disincentive for laid-off workers to find jobs immediately. The evidence suggests that many workers find jobs (miracle of miracles) when their unemployment benefits end. In tax-free America, all workers will be able to find jobs, maybe not in the field they would like immediately, but jobs will be available because there will always be consumer needs to fill in the marketplace, which means skilled, educated individuals will always be in demand.

A Free Economy is Reborn

By the year 2000, all taxes—coerced payments from taxpayers to government—will no longer exist. A tax-free America would not be any more utopian than the belief that taxes, government spending, and monetary inflation will reduce poverty, create prosperity, and curb or end the business cycle. It is utopian—and unrealistic—to believe that government power would be used wisely by public officials who have been elected to uphold the rights of the citizenry. As we have seen throughout history, Lord Acton's dictum cannot be ignored even in democratic "societies": "Power tends to corrupt, and absolute power corrupts absolutely."

The assertion, therefore, that *quasi-socialism*, government management of the economy, will lead the American people to the Promised Land has been shattered by experience. It is time for a major change, a break from the failed policies of the past five thousand years, worshipping the state as society's benefactor and problem solver.

Together the American people can build a society based on sound principles, and the principles that have stood the test of time—freedom and liberty. Although all public officials, intellectuals, and business leaders pay lip service to these principles, many support state coercion as a suitable and necessary means to organize society and build a prosperous economy. Instead, state-sanctioned plunder has replaced the principles of individual rights and economic freedom. The following timetable will thus once again restore freedom and liberty in America.

There will be several phases of the transition to *Tax-Free 2000*. Each phase will reduce government spending, ending the distortions of decades. A tax-free America will create an economy reflecting the American people's choices, not the desires of lobbyists and special interests. In fact, in a tax-free America there will be no lobbyists because there will be no public trough from which to feed! Government will be the number one protector of the people instead of the number one plunderer in society.

In phase one, the following immediate steps will be taken. Interest payments on the national debt will be suspended permanently so the federal government can balance its budget. All federal government departments, except Social Security, must reduce its spending 10–20 percent, thereby achieving a balanced budget in fiscal 1996. Interest rates will decline markedly as the federal government's credit demands end. As a result, abolishing the income tax in 1997 will greatly strengthen the economy as we head toward the twenty-first century.

During the transition, 1996 and 1997, local services, schools, libraries, recreational facilities, etc., will switch to a user fee system if they are not already using a fee-based system to deliver their services. In the suburbs, this will not pose a problem, because suburban families are more affluent in general than are urban households. Besides, if people do not support these activities, they will be expressing their dissatisfaction with the way one or more of the services are being delivered. The government agency (or agencies) will have to shape up inasmuch as it would no longer be able to depend on the "deep pockets" of taxpayers to support its inefficiencies. That would be real "entrepreneurial government!"

In urban centers, fees, contributions, donations, and endowments, will begin to support local public services in 1995 and 1996. In 1995, federal tax credits—dollar (or $1.10) for dollar—will be available so individuals and corporations would be able to make contributions to support these activities. In addition, a year later (1997), or sooner, the federal income tax will be abolished, and states with income taxes will extend the tax credit so funds could flow directly from taxpayers to the nonprofits. In 1998, state and local income taxes will be abolished, if not sooner, ending income taxation in the United States. Gasoline taxes, which are essentially user fees, will remain as long as the roads are maintained by local, state, and federal governments. If and when they are sold, innovative fee collection techniques will replace gasoline taxes.

In 1999, state and local sales taxes will be abolished, ending the distorting effects of this levy on production, consumption, and employment. At the federal level, all excise taxes will be terminated, including tariffs on imported goods, making the United States one gigantic free trade zone. Inexpensive goods will flow into the country, but more importantly, corporations will establish production here because of the country's tax-free status. The U.S. will become a mecca for corporations currently located in other countries, unless taxes are greatly reduced or eliminated throughout the world, thereby promoting a tax-free world!

In 1999, or sooner, local property taxes, which have been providing the revenue for funding local services, police, courts, streets, sanitation, sewers, and so forth will be abolished. Revenue for these services will be based on a rational pricing mechanism. Households that do not subscribe to the local police force, for example, would have their homeowners' insurance, renters' insurance and/or automobile insurance canceled because the risk of insuring such households and drivers without police protection would be high. In addition, what homeowner would risk having his home robbed and not be able to obtain police assistance to investigate the theft? However, if the property is mortgaged to the bank or finance company, these institutions would require police protection insurance just as these institutions currently require fire insurance. In short, contractual relationships will supplant coercion in society.

Additional Considerations

U. S. government employees, who will become former federal employees in 1996, have retirement plans with the federal government. These plans will be transferred to private retirement accounts as soon as possible. Employees will receive their contractual benefits according to a formula that does not place any burdens on the American people. For example, the assets in the trust accounts will be transferred to a private agency, insurance company, brokerage house, commercial bank, etc. Federal employees will use the accumulated assets to provide for their retirement income. If employees have invested in U.S. government bonds, they will receive the proceeds from asset sales to replace the federal securities. Whether the U.S. government securities will be replaced dollar for dollar is debatable, because the employees' other investment vehicle, common stock and corporate bonds, will dramatically increase in value over time, so there may be no need to replace most or all of the government's securities.

State, county, and local government employees will face the same situation. Their promised retirement benefits will be based on the performance of the investment portfolios the agencies will manage in a tax-free America. But, the fundamental principle must be adhered to, namely, former government employees will receive their retirement benefits without placing any burdens on the American people. With the economy booming, based on real productivity gains in the future, the increasing value of the portfolio will ensure sufficient revenue streams to former government workers in their retirement.

Foreign holders of U.S. government securities will have to bite the bullet. Foreigners have seen their U.S. bonds repudiated in the past by several states in the 1840s after the speculative boom of the 1830s caused by government misallocation of capital in wasteful public works projects. Rather than burden their citizens any further with interest payments and repayment of principal, several states, including Arkansas, repudiated their public debt. In 1971, President Nixon repudiated the last link between the dollar and gold when he forbid foreign holders of dollars from redeeming their dollars for gold. Foreigners have already experienced U.S. repudiation during the past 150 years. To restore the federal government's financial house, foreign holders of U.S. debt must once again see their bonds repudiated, an act which will restore not only the U.S. economy but the global economy as well.

The Future of Government

No reform of government would be complete without a discussion of the executive and legislative branches. In a tax-free America, the president, governors, and county executives would have an extremely limited role, namely, being chief executive and commander-in-chief of the military (in the case of the president) and their respective police forces. Inasmuch as crime is a local phenomenon, most police services will be handled by municipal and county police forces. Any state police would be confined to a coordinating role of county police services in order to capture fleeing suspects across a state. Otherwise, police functions will primarily be a local function.

The president of the United States will fundamentally be the commander of the armed services. The president will enunciate the principles of a free society and prevent any special interests from using government to plunder the people. As commander-in-chief, the president's duty will be to ensure that the American people are safe from foreign aggression. Without peace, the American people will not be able to have prosperity at home because more resources will be used for military purposes instead of civilian needs. Keeping the U.S. at peace requires that we do not become directly involved in foreign conflicts. Even the horrors of an internal conflict like we have seen in the former Yugoslavia cannot justify U.S. military intervention. The lessons of Vietnam must not be forgotten.

There are no simple solutions to civil wars and regional conflicts around the globe. But as a nation the United States must lead by example and not exercise military might to quell every disturbance in the world. Our civil war is a reminder of the bloody internal conflict we experienced. The United States paid a dear price for this dispute, and it would have probably been more horrible had there been active intervention by any of the European powers.

Thomas Jefferson stated an important principle for the United States nearly two hundred years ago. "Peace, commerce, and honest friendship with all nations—entangling alliances with none."[4]

The power of Congress and state legislatures must be circumscribed, because instead of representing the people against the sovereign, they have abandoned their traditional role and now represent the special interests against the people. To redress this imbalance the following reform guarantees that the legislature represents the people rather than engage in legal plunder.

Congress and the state legislatures will meet the first weekend of each month in their respective locations. Congress will meet to discuss military's preparedness to repel any and all attacks on the United States and to discuss the conflicts, if any, that exist around the world, and how the U.S. government could diplomatically offer assistance. Without the power to tax (the Sixteenth Amendment should be repealed just in case), Congress will oversee that the president is fulfilling his constitutional duty as commander-in-chief. The chief executive will be asked by the state legislatures and in county and municipal legislative bodies, to report on the administration of justice and the effectiveness of the police forces. Government will thus have its role limited to what it should have been doing through American history, protecting the people from criminals.

The president and other chief executives will be paid their present salaries but their staff will be drastically cut. The president will rely on the Joint Chiefs of Staff and his national security staff to monitor global events. Governors, county executives, and mayors will have virtually no staff except for liaisons with the police departments.

Members of Congress, state legislatures, and other bodies will be unpaid citizen representatives, a cross-section of the American people who will be working in their communities and then deliberating in the legislature once a month. The pensions of former legislators will be reduced sharply or eliminated completely. A new day in American politics will thus be born, the end of the career politician. Political campaigns will become nonevents because there will be no public trough from which to dispense the government's plunder. The electoral process will no longer be "lies, damned lies, and political promises." Campaigns will last a couple of months at most, September and October, instead of the seemingly endless campaigns the country currently experiences. In short, both major political parties will become extinct because they will no longer be able to argue about how to spend the people's money. In tax-free America, the people will spend their own money. Legal plunder will be abolished.

What is the likelihood of a tax-free America? The same likelihood that thirteen colonies had to form a free and independent nation more than two hundred years ago. The odds were great then, but the colonists succeeded in establishing the United States of America based on individual rights, a commodity-based money, and virtually no taxation. Today, the odds are great for dismantling the quasi-socialized economy, but a tax-free America will be a reality if the people want to build a sustainable, prosperous society. If the people choose to keep the status quo, they only have to blame themselves for the consequences of the next several years. A tax-free 2000, thus, is in the hands of 260 million Americans.

Epilogue

> The outlook is dark, but it is not entirely without hope. Here
> and there one can detect a break in the clouds. More and more
> people are becoming aware that the government has nothing to
> give them without first taking it away from somebody else—
> or from themselves ... There is real promise that public policy
> may be reversed before the damage from existing measures
> and trends has become irreparable.
>
> --Henry Hazlitt

How can the American dream be revived? The prescription is simple. Get a job, start a business, save for the future,
do charitable works, don't do drugs, don't have out-of-wedlock children (especially if you're a teenager), don't lobby for
subsidies, don't commit aggression against people nor steal
anyone's property. Becoming a productive, honest, non-self-
indulgent, law-abiding citizen is the key for human beings
establishing a "good" society. Proponents of big government,
however, vehemently disagree. They believe a good society is
reflected on how much government spends and taxes (redistributes the wealth of the citizenry). Citizenship requires that
an individual cooperate with his fellow citizens. If individuals
cannot be productive because they are afflicted with one of
many physical and/or mental disabilities, the enormous goodwill of their families, neighbors, and the general public will
assist them. After all, families voluntarily provide for their
children, the most dependent group in society. In rare instances where children are not cared for, appropriate measures
can be taken to place these children in a stable family. But, in
a society where people are forced, by law, to support other

228

individuals—whether they are wealthy, middle income, or poor— cannot survive in the long run. This is one of history's great lessons.

The American people need to become activists for economic freedom and liberty. Unfortunately, too many people are lobbyists for entitlements, the hallmark of our welfare system—socialism with a smile. However, when the vast majority of the American people demand an end to our mixed economy, a free economy will be reborn in the United States. Until that happy day returns, the proponents of free enterprise will have to battle the advocates of statism with better ideas.

Tax-Free 2000 offers several propositions. The idea that free enterprise is better than socialism (or semi-socialism); the idea that freedom is better than coercion; and the idea that liberty is better than tyranny. Who can object to these noble goals? If the American people want sustainable prosperity and government off their backs, the only social-economic system that will give us both material abundance and domestic tranquility is free enterprise. Under *laissez-faire*, the people will enjoy the fruits of their labor and will have to shoulder life's risks—the risk of losing a job, the risk of business failure, the risk of crop failure, the risk of floods, hurricanes, etc. People acting in concert voluntarily throughout the country will institute procedures and establish organizations to bear life's risks.

In a free America, government will no longer socialize risk. The socialization of risk is responsible for our $4 trillion national debt and $200+ billion annual federal deficits. When government spends money to prevent hardships for the unemployed, farmers, bank depositors, retirees, business owners, unwed mothers, and others, the funds have to come from the productive members of society either from taxes and/or loans. Since 1980, the U.S. Treasury has borrowed several trillion dollars from the American people and foreigners. This means that the federal government has not raised the revenue from the American people directly (taxation) to pay for each year's outlays. If this trend continues, federal budget deficits will reach dangerous levels in the years ahead. If borrowers become wary of lending Uncle Sam more money, the Federal Reserve could assist the U.S. Treasury fund the debt by purchasing a substantial portion of the federal government's securities. This is known as *monetizing the debt,* the printing of new money, which is the cause of inflation. If the deficit skyrockets in the 1990s, the Federal Reserve's purchase of the debt could lead to runaway inflation and a major disruption of economic activity.

We are nearing the end of the welfare state experiment in America. The collapse of the welfare state in both England and Sweden is a sober reminder to policymakers that the laws of economies cannot be repealed. The changes currently occurring in Sweden are so profound that as one Swedish political figure remarked in *Forbes* (24 May 1993): "Right now I'd rather be in Sweden than in the U.S., because we have seen the problems and are moving away from the welfare state. On your side, you are moving right into it, and you risk destroying your country."

Despite the collapse of both totalitarian socialism and democratic socialism, the ruling elite in Washington "just doesn't get it." An economic crisis has been in the making for eight decades, since the introduction of the income tax and the establishment of the Federal Reserve. Both the New Deal and Great Society greatly accelerated government intervention in the economy. The Clinton administration, meanwhile, wants to give us Act III of the drama that has been unfolding since the beginning of the century; big government without tears. In contrast, instead of repealing the welfare state, Republican administrations have tried to better manage big government in Washington. Unless there is a move to return the country to a limited government republic, the prognosis for the United States is for a major economic-financial crisis to occur in the near future unless we begin to take the road marked, Tax-Free 2000.

Trends can change but only if the people act. The people will act if they are "pressed to the wall," or if they passionately embrace principles because they care deeply about the future. One hundred years ago, a deep depression gripped the United States and the outcome was the agitation that eventually led to the passage of both the Sixteenth Amendment and the Federal Reserve System. In other words, the people accepted a short-term benefit (in this case a very fleeting gain)—lower tariffs—for income taxes on the wealthy. The "fox" thus entered the chicken coop. Taxation has reached intolerable levels in our country and government spending has climbed to the strato-sphere. The United States has indeed turned into a "planta-tion" where people look to the master in Washington to solve their problems. The American dream is teetering.

The American dream will be revived when the American people redeclare their independence. On April 15th or July 4th in Washington D.C., the American people need to join in solidarity and state in no uncertain terms: We want our independence—and tax dollars—back. We want a society based on free enterprise, freedom, and liberty. The Washing-ton elite will get the message because a powerful social movement cannot be ignored. If for some reason they don't get it, the American people have the ultimate weapons, the ballot box and the boycott. Boycott? Yes. If members of Congress refuse to reestablish a free economy, the American people could refuse to hire members of Congress or patronize their businesses when they retire if they "didn't do the right thing" in Washington. In other words, hit 'em in the pocketbook.

The battle lines are drawn. It is now up to the American people to determine if they want a free economy or a more socialized one as we enter the twenty-first century. If the people choose wisely, the twenty-first century will be the American Century. If the American people choose poorly, there will be no place to hide.

In the meantime, the American people need to stay informed about the ongoing assault on their income, wealth and freedoms. Organizations that produce outstanding articles, monographs, and books advocating economic freedom that I am most familiar with are:

The Cato Institute
1000 Massachusetts Ave. N.W.
Washington, D.C. 20001
202-842-0200

Citizens Against Government Waste
1301 Connecticut Ave. N.W., Ste. 400
Washington, D.C. 20036
202-441-4142

Citizens for a Sound Economy
470 L'Enfant Plaza East, S.W. #7112
Washington, D.C. 20024
202-488-8200

Competitive Enterprise Institute
233 Pennsylvania Ave. S.W. #22
Washington, D.C. 20003
202-547-1010

Foundation for Economic Education
30 S. Broadway
Irvington-on-Hudson, NY 10533
914-591-7230

Foundation for Rational Economics and Education
837 Plantation Dr.
Clute, TX 77531
409-265-3034

Future of Freedom Foundation
P.O. Box 11350 Random Hills Road, Suite 800
Fairfax, VA 22030
703-934-6101

The Independent Institute
134 Ninety-Eight Avenue
Oakland, CA 94603

Institute for Humane Studies
4400 University Drive
Fairfax, VA 22030-444
703-323-1055

Laissez Faire Books
942 Howard St.
San Francisco, CA 94103
800-326-0996
415-541-9780

Ludwig Von Mises Institute
Mises Building
Auburn, AL 26849
205-844-2500

National Center for Policy Analysis
12655 North Central Expressway #726
Dallas, TX 75243
214-386-6272

National Taxpayers Union
325 Pennsylvania Ave. S.E.
Washington, D.C. 20003
202-543-2300

Pacific Research Institute
177 Post Street #500
San Francisco, CA 94108
415-989-0833

Write to them, call them, obtain information from them that you can use to discuss with friends, colleagues and family members. Then write brief letters to and articles for the local newspaper. Freedom is within our grasp—we cannot afford to let it slip away!

There are literally hundreds of other organizations working for economic freedom and lower taxes. The best single source of these organizations is *The Right Guide*, published by Economic America, Inc., 612 Church Street, Ann Arbor, MI 48104, (313) 995-0865.

Finally, protecting your hard-earned assets in a period of increasing confiscation by the government becomes more and more difficult. Due to the potential reimposition of the Bullion Confiscation Order of 1933, two individuals who have been offering advice to average citizens throughout the country for many years on how to protect their wealth are:

North American Trading
Attn: Jack Weber
13951 North Scottsdale Rd. Ste. 215
Scottsdale, AZ 85254
800-877-9799

Camino Coin Co.
Attn: Burt Blumert
875 Mahler Rd.
Burlingame, CA 94010
800-348-8001
415-348-3000

Throughout history, freedom and liberty—the natural social conditions of human beings—have been in relatively short supply. Liberty exists only when the people demand it. We are witnessing a retreat from statism and the embrace of free enterprise throughout the world. As the twentieth century draws to a close, the American people have the opportunity to once again declare their independence and proclaim liberty throughout the land. What could be more glorious than participating in America's Second Revolution for economic freedom and liberty?

Notes

Chapter 1

[1] Robert Higgs, *The Transformation of the American Economy, 1865–1914* (New York: John Wiley & Sons, 1971), 2–3.

[2] Ibid., 123.

[3] John F. Witte, *The Politics and Development of the Federal Income Tax* (Madison, Wisconsin: University of Wisconsin Press, 1985), 67.

[4] See Charles Hoffman, *The Depression of the Nineties: An Economic History* (Westport, Connecticut: Greenwood Publishing Corporation, 1970) for a comprehensive review of this period.

[5] Robert Higgs, *Crisis and Leviathan: Critical Episodes in the Growth of American Government* (New York: Oxford University Press, 1987), 98.

[6] Burton W. Folsom, Jr., *The Myth of the Robber Barons* (Herndon, Virginia: Young America's Foundation, 1991), ix–x.

[7] Ibid., 123–124.

[8] Ibid., 87.

[9] Dominick T. Armentano, *Antitrust and Monopoly: Anatomy of a Policy Failure*, 2nd ed., (New York: Holmes & Meirer Publishers Inc., 1990), 65.

[10] Ibid., 58.

[11] Ibid., 67. See Armentano's critique of the government's prosecution of Standard Oil as an example of the changing winds regarding business practices in the early twentieth century.

[12] See Gabriel Kolko, *The Triumph of Conservatism: A Reinterpretation of American History, 1900-1916* (New York: The Free Press, 1963), 129ff.

[13] Folsom, *The Myth* , 17–22.

[14] Ibid., 23ff.

[15] Albro Martin, *James J. Hill and the Opening of the Northwest* (New York: Oxford University Press, 1976), 253.

[16] Ibid., 29.

[17] Ibid, 35.

[18] See Gabriel Kolko's *Railroads and Regulation: 1877-1916* (Princeton: Princeton University Press, 1965) for an excellent discussion of the relationship between the railroads and government policies.

[19] Ron Paul and Lewis Lehrman, *The Case for Gold: A Minority Report of the U. S. Gold Commission* (Washington D. C.: Cato Institute, 1982), 110.

[20] Higgs, *Crisis and Leviathan*, 113–114.

Chapter 2

[1] Carolyn Webber and Aaron Wildavsky, *A History of Taxation and Expenditure in the Western World* (New York: Simon and Schuster, 1986), 43.

[2] Frank Chodorov, *The Income Tax: Root of All Evil*, with a Foreword by J. Bracken Lee (Old Greenwich, Connecticut: Devin-Adair Company, 1954).

[3] Charles Adams, *Fight, Flight and Fraud: The Story of Taxation* (Curacao: Euro-Dutch Publishers, 1982), 17.

[4] Webber and Wildavsky, *A History of Taxation*, 68.

[5] Adams, *Fight*, 21.

[6] Ibid., 31.

[7] Webber and Wildavsky, *A History of Taxation*, 88.

[8] Adams, *Fight*, 43.

[9] Ibid., 49.

[10] Webber and Wildavsky, *A History of Taxation*, 103–104 and Adams, *Fight*, 45.

[11] Adams, *Fight*, 50-51.

[12] Ibid., 53.

[13] M. Rostovtzeff, *The Social and Economic History of the Hellenistic World*, 2nd ed., vol. I (London: Oxford University Press, 1952), 443.

[14] Adams, *Fight*, 54.

[15] Ibid., 94.

[16] Ibid., 57.

[17] Ibid., 62.

[18] Ibid., 63.

[19] Ibid., 68.

[20] Ibid., 71.

[21] Ibid., 76.

[22] Webber and Wildavsky, *A History of Taxation*, 143.

[23] M. Rostovtzeff, *The Social and Economic History of the Roman Empire*, 2nd ed., vol. I (London: Oxford University Press, 1952), 530.

[24] Webber and Wildavsky, *A History of Taxation*, 149.

[25] Ibid.

[26] Nathan Rosenberg and L. E. Birdzell, Jr., *How the West Grew Rich:*

The Economic Transformation of the Industrial World (New York: Basic Books, Inc., 1986), 56.

[27] Webber and Wildavsky, *A History of Taxation,* 161.

[28] Ibid., 165. Also see Robert S. Lopez, *The Commercial Revolution of the Middle Ages, 950-1350* (Englewood Cliffs, New Jerseyt: Prentice Hall, Inc., 1971) for an insightful discussion of Europe's economic development.

[29] Ibid., 175.

[30] Adams, *Fight,* 121.

[31] Ibid., 131.

[32] Ibid., 124.

[33] This was especially true during the period 1348–1500. See Howard L. Adelson, *Medieval Commerce* (Princeton, New Jersey: D. Van Nostrand Company, Inc., 1962), 88 ff.

[34] E. L. Jones, *The European Miracle: Environments, Economies, and the Geopolitics in the History of Europe and Asia,* 2nd ed. (New York: Cambridge University Press, 1987), 185–186, 197–198.

[35] Florin Aftalion, *The French Revolution: An Economic Interpretation,* trans. Martin Thom (Cambridge, England: Cambridge University Press, 1990), 11.

[36] Murray N. Rothbard, *Conceived in Liberty,* vol. l: *The American Colonies in the 17th Century* (New Rochelle, New York: Arlington House Publishers, 1975), 171.

[37] Ibid., 82.

[38] Ibid., 84.

[39] Ibid., 85.

[40] Ibid., 96.

[41] Ibid., 101–102.

[42] Ibid., 402.

[43] Murray N. Rothbard, *Conceived in Liberty,* vol. II: *"Salutary Neglect": The American Colonies in the First Half of the 18th Century* (New Rochelle, New York: Arlington House Publishers, 1975), 268.

[44] Ibid., 205.

[45] Adams, *Fight,* 232.

[46] Joseph Dorfman, *The Economic Mind in American Civilization,* vol. 3: 1865–1918, reprint ed. (New York: Augustus M. Kelley, 1969), 55.

[47] Ibid., 162.

[48] John F. Witte, *The Politics and Development of the Federal Income Tax* (Madison, Wisconsin: University of Wisconsin Press, 1985), 73.

[49] Arthur A. Ekrich, "The Sixteenth Amendment: The Historical

Background," *Cato Journal*, I (Spring, 1982): 170.

[50] James Ring Adams, *Secrets of the Tax Revolt* (New York: Harcourt Brace Jovanovich, 1984), 33, 34.

[51] Ekrich, *Cato*, 177.

[52] Ibid., 177.

[53] Webber and Wildavsky, *A History of Taxation*, 422.

[54] John D. Buenker, "The Ratification of the Federal Income Tax Amendment," *Cato Journal*, I (Spring 1982): 184.

[55] Ibid., 188.

[56] Ibid., 195.

[57] Ibid., 196.

[58] Ibid., 202.

[59] Webber and Wildavsky, *A History of Taxation*, 121.

[60] Higgs, *Crisis and Leviathan*, 114–115.

[61] Chodorov, *The Income*, 40.

[62] Ibid.

Chapter 3

[1] Frederic Bastiat, *The Law*, trans. Dean Russell (Irvington-on-Hudson, New York: Foundation for Economic Education, Inc., 1984), 21.

[2] Chris Edwards, *Special Report: Tax Freedom Day 1993 is May 3,*(Washington, D.C.: Tax Foundation, April 1993).

[3] *Barron's: National Business and Financial Weekly* 121 (22 April 1991): 28.

[4] James L. Payne, "Unhappy Returns: The $600-Billion Tax Ripoff,' *Policy Review* 59 (Winter 1992): 21.

[5] Bastiat, *The Law,* 12.

Chapter 4

[1] Samuel L. Blumenfeld, *Is Public Education Necessary?* (Old Greenwich, Connecticut: Devin-Adair, 1981, reprint ed., Boise, Idaho: The Paradigm Company, 1985), 18.

[2] Myron Lieberman, *Privitization and Educational Choice* (New York: St. Martin's Press, 1989), 278.

[3] See the six-part series "Rethinking Welfare," *New York Times,*(July 5 to July 26, 1992).

[4] Clifford F. Thies, "Bring Back the Poorhouse and the Workhouse,"

The Free Market, (10 October 1992): 6.

[5] Steve Steckler and Lavinia Payson, "Infrastructure," *Privatization for New York: Competing for a Better Future*, <u>A Report of the New York Senate Advisory Commission on Privatization</u>, Ronald S. Lauder, Chairman, (January 1992).

[6] David Osborne and Ted Gaebler, *Reinventing Government: How the Entrepreneurial Spirit is Transforming the Public Sector* (New York: Addison-Wesley Publishing Company, Inc., 1992), 60.

[7] William Tucker, *The Excluded Americans: Homelessness and Housing Policies* (Washington, D.C.: Regnery Gateway, 1990), 180.

[8] Ibid., 181–182.

[9] Ibid.

[10] Ibid., 183.

[11] E. S. Savas, *Privatization: The Key to Better Government* (Chatham, New Jersey: Chatham House Publishers, Inc., 1987), 200.

[12] Steckler and Payson, *Privatization for New York*, 247,248.

[13] Tucker, *Excluded*, 286ff.

[14] Ibid., 300.

Chapter 5

[1] "The Forgotten Public at Large," *Investor's Business Daily* (3 September 1992): 2.

[2] Quoted in "A Post Cold War Defense Plan Maps a Smaller but Ready Force," *Wall Street Journal*, (8 February 1994): A12.

[3] "Whipping the Deficit," *The Record* (10 July 1991): E-2.

[4] Peter J. Ferrara, *Social Security: Averting the Crisis* (Washington, D.C.: Cato Institute, 1982), 6.

[5] Alice M. Rivlin, *Reviving the American Dream: The Economy, the States and the Federal Government* (Washington, D.C.: The Brookings Institution, 1992), 171.

[6] "New York's Medicaid Costs Surge, But Health Care for the Poor Lags," *New York Times*(14 April 1991): sec. 1, 1.

Chapter 6

[1] Murray N. Rothbard, *The Case for a 100 Percent Gold Dollar* (Auburn, Alabama: Ludwig von Mises Institute, 1991), 23. Professor Rothbard's discussion of gold, money, and fractional reserve banking in this essay originally appeared in *In Search of a Monetary Constitu-*

tion, edited by Leland B. Yeager (Cambridge, Massachusetts: Harvard University Press, 1962).

[2] Murray N. Rothbard, *What Has Government Done to Our Money* (Auburn, Alabama: Ludwig von Mises Institute, 1990), 34. This monograph was originally published in 1963 and is one of the best introductions to money and banking.

[3] Gabriel Kolko, *The Triumph of Conservatism: A Reinterpretation of American History, 1900-1916* (New York: The Free Press, 1963), 4.

[4] Ron Paul and Lewis Lehrman, *The Case for Gold: A Minority Report of the U.S. Gold Commission* (Washington, D.C.: Cato Institute, 1982), 120.

[5] Murray N. Rothbard, *The Mystery of Banking* (New York: Richardson & Snyder, 1983) 235.

[6] Murray N. Rothbard, *America's Great Depression*, 4th edition (New York: Richardson & Snyder, 1983) 282.

[7] Ludwig von Mises, *Human Action: A Treatiste on Economics*, 3rd revised edition (Chicago: Henry Regnery Company, 1966), 572.

[8] Elgin Groseclose, *America's Money Machine: A Story of The Federal Reserve* (Westport, Connecticut: Arlington House Publishers, 1980), 255.

Chapter 7

[1] *The Oxford Dictionary of Quotations*, 3rd Edition (New York: Oxford University Press, 1980), 272.

[2] See Murray N. Rothbard's discussion of making the dollar as good as gold in *The Mystery of Banking*, 263-269.

[3] Ludwig von Mises, "Inflation and You," *Economic Freedom and Interventionism*, ed. Bettina Bien Greaves (Irvington-on-Hudson, New York: Foundation for Economic Education, Inc., 1990), 88,89.

Chapter 8

[1] James L. Payne, "Unhappy Returns: The $600-Billion Tax Ripoff," *Policy Review* 59 (Winter 1992): 24.

[2] Ibid.

[3] Ibid.

[4] *Oxford Dictionary*, 272.